Anna Maude Bower

The Sources and Text of Richard Wagner's Opera

Anna Maude Bower

The Sources and Text of Richard Wagner's Opera

ISBN/EAN: 9783337386658

Printed in Europe, USA, Canada, Australia, Japan

Cover: Foto ©Thomas Meinert / pixelio.de

More available books at **www.hansebooks.com**

THE SOURCES AND TEXT

OF

RICHARD WAGNER'S OPERA

DIE MEISTERSINGER VON NÜRNBERG'

A DISSERTATION

PRESENTED

TO THE FACULTY OF CORNELL UNIVERSITY FOR THE DEGREE
OF DOCTOR OF PHILOSOPHY

BY

ANNA MAUDE BOWEN, PH. B.

MUNICH
PUBLICATION OF DR. H. LÜNEBURG, MAXIMILIANSPL. 3.
1897.

To my mother

this essay is gratefully

dedicated.

PREFATORY NOTE.

The material for this thesis has been collected partly at Cornell University and partly abroad, in the libraries of Munich and Leipsic. Cordial acknowledgements are due Prof. Dr. Franz Muncker, of the University of Munich, Prof. Dr. Karl von Bahder, of the University of Leipsic, Prof. C. H. Elson, ~~Director of~~ the New England Conservatory of Music, and to the firm of B. Schott's Sons, Mayence, as well as to all members of my examining committee, for suggestions and information.

Leipsic, 3 March, 1897.

ANNA MAUDE BOWEN.

INTRODUCTION.

I. MINNESONG AND MASTERSONG.

The question as to the relation of Minnesong to Mastersong has long been settled, and even the dust of the unequal conflict between Docen and Jacob Grimm has cleared away.[1]) We know now that the Minnesong was the living blossom, the Mastersong the curious fossil, of the same poetic growth. The Mastersingers themselves had an indistinct perception of this fact, for they made some of the legendary founders and first masters of their art old and famous Minnesingers. Wagner has utilized this connection by bringing into juxtaposition the virile and the sterile, the spontaneous and the formal, Walther and Beckmesser, leaving us to draw by inference our own poetic moral. We shall examine more closely the development of this relation.

Grimm tells us[2]) that as soon as a national poetry loses its objective character it goes over into a glaring subjectivity, a change marked by the tendency toward lyric and artificial forms. The „natural, simple, national, epic"[3]) disappears, and from that time on the effort of advancing culture is ever „to unite the lost epic with the lyric, i. e. te approach the dramatic principle ... the greatest triumph of complete culture and the highest poetic element".[4]) Thus, after the decadence of the national epic in Germany, Minnesong and Mastersong arose simultaneously, „the one [term] denoting the content, the other the form".[5]) This

---

1) For Grimm's dictum see „Ueber den altdeutschen Meistergesang". For his account of this entire controversy see same book, 13 ff.
2) „Kleinere Schriften", IV, 13.
3) Ibid. IV, 13.
4) Ibid. IV, 13.
5) Ibid. IV, 13.

poetry was confined to the stronger and more independent part of the nation, that is, to the nobility, for the first two centuries and a half of its existence (1143—1400), but when the nobility declined, it passed into the hands of the ever increasingly powerful citizen-class, there living on two centuries longer (1400—1600). The Minnesong originated in the golden age of the Hohenstaufens, and bears the imprint of that knightly spirit, that deep religious fervor, and that extravagant worship of woman which characterize this period. To the two characteristics first mentioned we owe the third, for the crusading knight who fought to free the Holy Land from the terrible Turk was fired by the inspiration of the Mary-cult, the germ of his wider veneration for woman. This admiration for woman was no new thing in Germany. From the time when the author of the Annales tells us of the Germans that they regarded their women as sanctum aliquid et providum [1]), through the era of the Nibelungenlied and of Gudrun, she was held in constant reverence, until Christianity, bringing with it the conception of the sinless mother of God, effected an increase of veneration which amounted to a cult.

Thus inspired arose the Minnesingers, that melodious choir of poets who keep their heritage of renown even unto this day. Their songs of spring and love, so sincere, so naïve, still breathe the odorous freshness of long-past joyance and delight. Thus sympathetically are they characterized by D'Assailly:[2])

„Les Minnesinger chantent la nature avec la candeur des petits enfants qui s'élancent en souriant dans le bras de leur mère. Ils font leurs chefs d'oeuvre comme le moissonneur fait sa garbe, sans y songer; et ne se retournent pas pour voir s'ils sont suivis de cette glaneuse qu'on nomme la postérité. Ils sont voués à Dieu, à la Vierge, aux femmes, à la patrie. Une passion jeune et tendre les anime et pénètre leur parole d'une sorte de parfum, mais cette passion est candide, et, loin de rechercher le bruit des villes ou le faste des cours, elle est amoureuse de solitude, de recueillement, de mystère. . . . La voix du monde

---
1) Tacitus: „Germania", § VIII.
2) „Les Chevaliers-Poëtes de l'Allemagne", 12 ff.

effraye les Minnesinger, la marche des passants les inquiète comme les oiseaux dans la saison des nids.[1] ... Ils sont simples, ils sont vrais plus qu'on ne saurait le dire. Leur esprit se remplit sans cesse de pensées riantes et limpides. ... La plupart ont un style qui leur est propre, une doleur de prédilection, des tournures originales, une idée dont ils s'épreuvent aussi bien que de leur dame. ... Novateurs dans un siècle turbulent, nos poëtes ont été les premiers à sentir qu'un hymne d'amour vaut bien un bardit de guerre. ... Qu'on ne s'attende pas à trouver des savants dans les Minnesinger ... la plupart ont beaucoup plus étudié dans les champs que dans les livres."

Add to this a sentence from Grimm:[2] „Unter andern ist offenbar, dass nie eine Poesie frauenhafter gewesen, als diese war, mit ihrer unermüdlichen Blumenliebe, mit ihrem stillen Glänzen", and our characterization is complete.

Minnesong was in its prime in the first quarter of the thirteenth century, when Walther von der Vogelweide, Hartmann von Aue, Wolfram von Eschenbach and Gottfried von Strassburg were all yet living. After the tragic death of the last of the Hohenstaufens, however, came about the gradual decay of knightly poetry.

„Die Fürsten ermüden der Minnelieder nach und nach, das Volk kann sie nicht brauchen. Die Meister klagen über den Verfall des höfischen Sangs, die Loblieder auf die Fürsten und Herren gerathen immer häufiger, schmeichelnder und gezierter, je schlechter sie bezahlt werden, und sie unterlassen dabei nie zu sagen, dass ihr Lob ein wahres sey und sie das der Schlechten verabscheuen."[3]

The end of the thirteenth century introduced „die kaiserlose, die schreckliche Zeit", followed by the autocratic rule of the Habsburgs, dark ages for Germany in very truth. The nobles became mere robber-knights, and at neither castle nor court was there welcome for the singer.

---

1) D'Assailly appears purposely to omit all mention of the political poems of the Minnesingers.
2) „Ueber den altdeutschen Meistergesang", 8.
3) Ibid. 31.

The later Minnesingers indulge in extravagant vagaries of both content and verse. It is a significant fact that Frauenlob, to whom the Mastersingers referred the foundation of their first School, was one those singers who played with artificial verseforms to the havoc of his subject.[1]

But in the middle of the fifteenth century torpid Europe was aroused. Through the capture of Constantinople by the Turks and the almost simultaneous invention of printing came, for Germany at least, the era of Humanism and the Reformation.[2]

The imperial cities had been steadily growing in importance, and soon became the centers of all culture. Who but the honest burghers began now to flirt with the shy Muse, as they looked about for recreation after their day's labor? And although they clipped the wings of their Pegasus, and trained him to amble along in harness withal, yet they had taken him out of pound, and they cherished him fondly until he was ready for a new flight. From the fifteenth century on, the time of court-life and wandering for this poetry was past.

„Denn es hatten die Fürsten den Meistersingern alle Gunst entzogen, und auf andere Stände konnten sie eine Einwirkung nicht erneuern, die sie nie gehabt. Dagegen gerieth die Kunst in den Bürgerstand allmälig herab, nicht als ob vorher keine Bürger derselben theilhaftig gewesen, sondern weil jetzo eine Menge aus diesem Stand sie umfassten und blühender als je machten, wenn man auf die Anzahl der Ausübenden sieht. Nirgends hätte der sinkende Meistergesang so lange gehalten, wenn er nicht in die deutschen Städte gelangt wäre, wo die wohlhabenden Bürger es sich zur Ehre ersahen, dass sie die Kunst einiger ihrer Vorfahrer nicht ausgehen liessen, und bald war sie durch eine Menge Theilnehmer in Anspruch und Förmlichkeit gesichert."[3]

Many of the old Minnesingers were called Masters; Veldeke

---

1) Grimm: „Ueber den altdeutschen Meistergesang", 32. — „Frauenlob's Werke sind überreich wunderbar und von einer Verworrenheit, aus der sie sich gleichsam zu ihrem eigenen Schmerz nicht zu lösen vermögen."
2) cf. Wilsing: „Die Meistersinger von Nürnberg", 2 ff.
3) „Ueber den altdeutschen Meistergesang", 33.

is so called by Gottfried of Strassburg. At all events, with the beginning of the thirteenth century there were rules and Masters enough.¹) The famous War of the Wartburg was, according to Müller,²) only a sort of Singing-school.

The oldest Singing-school of which we have any account was founded in Mainz by Frauenlob (Heinrich von Meissen). Frauenlob is now celebrated, first, for his famous poetic encounter with Barthel Regenbogen in regard to the greater dignity of the title Frau or Weib, in which he upheld the superiority of the former (hence probably the name by which he is best known), and secondly, for the quaint record of the Latin chronicler³) in regard to his burial:

"Anno Domini MCCCXVII⁴) in vigilia Sancta Andreæ sepultus est Henricus dictus Frauenlob, in Maguntia, in ambitu majoris ecclesiæ, juxta scholas honorifice valde: qui deportatus fuit a mulieribus ab hospitio usque ad locum sepulturæ, et lamentationes et querelæ maximæ anditæ fuerunt ab eis, propter laudes infinitas, quas imposuit omni generi fæmineo in dictaminibus suis. Tantæ etiam ibi copia fuit vini fusa in sepulchrum suum, quod circumfluebat per totum ambitum ecclesiæ. Cantica canticorum dictavit teutonice quæ vulgariter dicuntur Unser Frauen Lied, e multa alia bona."

Well might the ladies weep and pour libations of wine into his tomb, for he was the last of the old Minnesingers, vowed to their service, as well as the first of the Mastersingers.

II. ORIGIN AND DEVELOPMENT OF MASTERSONG.

As regards the origin of their art, the Mastersingers had a proud legend which Wagenseil discredits, but relates as follows:⁵)

---

1) Grimm: „Ueber den altdeutschen Meistergesang", 30.
2) Müller: „Die Meistersinger von Nürnberg", 14.
3) Urstisius: „Germaniæ historici illustres" etc., II, 108.
4) Frauenlob died 1318. See Uhland: „Geschichte der Dichtung und Sage", II, 293 note.
5) Wagenseil: „Buch von der Meister-Singer Holdseligen Kunst" etc., a supplement to his „De Civitate Noribergensi Commentatio", 503.

„The Mastersingers themselves have a very erroneous opinion, namely, that their art originated first in Germany in the time of the Emperor Otto I., and that moreover through XII gifted men, its undoubted devisers, as well as through the divine ordinance, since no one of them knew aught of the other. These men were called:[1]) 1. Heinrich Frauenlob, Doctor of the Holy Scriptures at Mainz. 2. Heinrich Mögeling, Doctor of the Holy Scriptures at Prague. 3. Nicolaus Klingsohr, Master of the Liberal Arts. 4. Der starcke Poppo, otherwise also called der starke Poppser, a glass-burner. 5. Walther von der Vogelweide, a country gentleman. 6. Wolfgang Rohn or Rahm, a knight.[2]) 7. Hannss Ludwig Marner, a nobleman. 8. Barthel Regenbogen, a smith. 9. Sigmar the Wise, otherwise called der Römer von Zwickau.[3]) 10. Conrad Geiger, whom others call Jäger, of Würtzburg, a musician.[4]) 11. N. Cantzler, a fisherman. 12. Steffan Stoll, otherwise known as der alte Stoll, a ropemaker."

The Mastersingers were evidently proud of the noble names in this list. Wagenseil says[5]) that the Mastersong was devised first „by most wise and learned people, as Doctors, knights and barons, nobles and other wise people, rich and poor". Puschman says also:[6]) „And this art is to be held as especially dear and worthy on this account, that it is of exalted, noble origin, being first devised by excellent noble people." It is interesting to note that „der starke Poppo", who is Master of the Seven Liberal Arts in Schilter and Puschman, becomes a tradesman in Wagenseil, a change which may perhaps show a tendency in

---

1) Other lists substantially the same are in Schilter: „Thesaurus Antiquitatum Teutonicarum", III, 88, and Puschman: „Gründtlicher Bericht des Deudschen Meistergesangs", reprinted in „Neudrucke deutscher Litteraturwerke des XVI. und XVII. Jahrhunderts", 4.
2) Wolfram von Eschenbach. See Schilter, III, 88.
3) Reinmar von Zweter.
4) Schilter, III, 88 gives his name as Conrad von Würzburg, ein Geiger am Hof.
5) „Von der Meister-Singer Holdseligen Kunst", 521.
6) „Gründtlicher Bericht", 4.

the later times to make the art more completely, even in its origin, a possession of the Burgher-class.

Wagenseil continues his story:[1])
„Of these they say that, because they rebuked the evil life and conduct of the pope and clergy, they were accused at first before Pope Leo VIII as heretics who were introducing new and false doctrines. In consequence of this therefore the Emperor, while in Italy, summoned the XII Mastersingers at first to Pavia, at the earnest solicitation of the Pope, and later, when he had gone from Italy into France, summoned them likewise to Paris;[2]) and since in both of these places, in the presence of the Emperor, of the pope's legates, and also of many scholars and men of rank they not only gave glorious specimens of their gracious art, to the satisfaction of all, but also completely removed all false presumption of their heresy, — their newly devised art was approved and praised by both emperor and pope, as well as endowed with privileges, and they were exhorted diligently to persevere therein."

Wagenseil then devotes four pages to the same account as given in a Mastersong dating from the beginning of the sixteenth century.[3]) **Puschman**, who wrote more than a century before **Wagenseil**, gives the date of the trial, Anno Christi 692.[4]) **Grimm** regards the whole story as a myth, and with justice.[5]) **Wagenseil** notes the incongruity in dates between the reign of Otto I and the death of **Frauenlob**,[6]) and **Puschman** himself must have had an inkling that something was wrong in his chronology, for he arbitrarily changes Otto I to

---

1) „Von der Meister-Singer Holdseligen Kunst", 503.
2) This double locality of the trial, i. e. Pavia and Paris, is evidently **Wagenseil**'s attempt to reconcile two stories. **Puschman**, 4 gives Paris as the scene of the trial, the Strassburg Tablature, as also the Mastersong quoted by **Wagenseil** 505, Pavia. **Schilter** says of his account, „Nihil antiquius obtineri potui". We have no reason for supposing that the trial took place at Paris.
3) Uhland: „Geschichte der Dichtung und Sage", II, 286.
4) „Gründtlicher Bericht", 4.
5) „Ueber den altdeutschen Meistergesang", 115 ff.
6) „Von der Meister-Singer Holdseligen Kunst", 509.

Otto II in his second edition¹), a correction which profits little. To quote Uhland:²)

„Anachronismen fehlen freilich dieser Sage nicht. Der geringste darunter ist, dass Leo VIII. im Jahr 962 noch nicht den päpstlichen Stuhl bestiegen hatte. Aber auch von den sämtlichen Dichtern, deren Namen in die Zwölfzahl gesammelt sind, fällt keiner in die Zeit Otto's I. und Leo's VIII., und ebensowenig sind sie grossenteils unter sich gleichzeitig. ... Der älteste, Walther von der Vogelweide, gehört dem Anfang des 13. Jahrhunderts, Frauenlob mit mehreren Andern dem Schlusse desselben und Heinrich von Müglin dem weit vorgerückten 14. Jahrhundert an."

From Otto also they claimed to have received a golden crown³), with which to adorn the victor in song, and this crown was the central ornament of the coat-of-arms of the Mastersingers at Mainz. This city was „at once the High-school and the place of Assembly of the Mastersingers, whither those betook themselves, who desired to learn that art beyond all others. There were securely preserved the privileges and prerogatives which the societies received from time to time from the Roman emperors, especially the golden crown of the Emperor Otto ... and the letter with the Mastersingers' coat-of-arms".⁴).

The number twelve had no doubt a mystic signification. Metzger⁵) compares the twelve old Masters to the twelve apostles, and the schools of Nuremberg and Augsburg⁶) had also twelve Masters selected from their own number, as we shall have occasion to note. There is no doubt a reference in the number to the twelve heroes in the Rose Garden at Worms. The garden also played an important part in the Mastersingers symbolism. One of the tablets which was hung up to announce meetings of the Nuremberg School had painted on it a garden

---

1) Grimm: „Ueber den altdeutschen Meistergesang", 118.
2) „Geschichte der Dichtung und Sage", 286 f.
3) Schilter, III, 88; Wagenseil, 492; Puschman, 4.
4) Wagenseil, 515.
5) Grimm: „Ueber den altdeutschen Meistergesang", 120, note.
6) Uhland: „Geschichte der Dichtung und Sage", II, 288.

in which were several persons wandering about. Above it was the verse:[1])
„Zwölff Alte Männer vor viel Jahren,
Thäten den Garten wohl bewahren,
Vor wilden Thieren, Schwein, und Beeren
Die wolten ihn verwüsten gern;
Die lebten, als man zehlt verwahr,
Neunhundert und 62 Jahr."

Wagenseil goes on to explain:[2])

„That the garden was brought to mind, comes about probably on account of the Rose-Garden at Worms, so highly renowned in ancient times, wherein the bravest and strongest heroes of the world were wont to contend and to let their prowess be seen. ... Just as if, as the heroes had striven for precedence with undismayed courage and with all the might of their bodies, so the Mastersingers strove also for the honor of their intellect and of their skill in the art of song."

Hans Sachs, in his „Schulkunst",[3]) compares Mastersong to a garden also, and Puschman quotes a Mastersong which makes use of the same figure.[4])

So much for the rise of the Mastersong! From Mainz it spread throughout the cities of southern Germany, flourishing especially at Nuremberg and Strasburg.[5]) „Im vierzehnten Jahrhundert blüht er zu Mainz, Strassburg, Colmar, Frankfurt, Wirtzburg, Zwickau, Prag. Im funfzehnten zu Nürnberg, Augsburg. Im sechszehnten zu Regensburg, Ulm, München, Steiermark, Mähren (Iglau), Breslau, Görliz bis nach Danzig. Im siebenzehnten zu Memmingen, Basel, Dünkelspiel."[6]) The Augs-

---

1) Wagenseil, 541.
2) Ibid. 541.
3) Sachs: „Dichtungen", in „Deutsche Dichter des sechszehnten Jahrhunderts", 10, 102 ff. Ranisch, 259 thinks that this reference to a garden quoted in Wagenseil may go back also to this same song by Sachs.
4) „Gründtlicher Bericht", 46 f.
5) Wagenseil, 515.
6) Grimm: „Ueber den altdeutschen Meistergesang", 129.

burg School was regularly established in 1450,[1]) that at Strasburg about 1492.[2]) Mastersong was most prosperous in the middle of the fifteenth century. At the end of the sixteenth century it began to decline. As everything else in Germany, it suffered severely from the Thirty Years' War, and from that time led only a precarious existence into our own century. In 1839 the School at Ulm dissolved, giving its insignia to the Ulm „Liederkranz", but it was not until 1844 that Mastersong ceased to exist in Germany, by the formal dissolution of the Memmingen School.[3])

III. THE HISTORICAL VALUE OF THE MASTERSINGERS' ART.

In his seventh chapter[4]) Wagenseil treats of the advantages and uses of the Mastersingers' art, somewhat as follows.

In the first place, since the Mastersingers took their subjects largely from the Bible, it served to make that book more familiar. It conduced to the safety of the state, since it united the citizens, and established peace and quiet. It prevented the jealousy which often existed between different trades-guilds, for its members were taken from all these guilds. It also took the place of more questionable amusements, and reduced the evils of idleness. Hear Wagenseil again:[5])

„But no one celebrates fewer holidays than the good Mastersingers, for when they have worked hard and fast the whole day to win their bread, and now the eve of rest has come, while other tradesmen go into beer-houses or elsewhere together, these men sit down, compose new poems, repeat the old Tunes, write great books of songs, or instruct their apprentices, that the art may not perish. It is really a matter to wonder at, that the dear folks take upon themselves such great pains and labor, without the slighest advantage from it; for all that they do is

---

1) Mey: „Der Meistergesang in Geschichte und Kunst," 6.
2) Schilter, III, 89.
3) No new „Tune" had, however, been invented since 1788. See Mey, 14.
4) Wagenseil, 559 ff.
5) Ibid. 560 ff.

merely out of love toward the German Fatherland, and toward that gracious old Art, in order that it may be handed down to their posterity as they received it from their ancestors. Elsewhere the saying „Marcet sine praemio Virtus, et nemo gratis bonus est" is valid, but here no reward can be expected. ...

I am completely of the opinion that the Mastersingers Guild makes for the great renown and honor, first, of the few Imperial cities in which this art is now practiced, and then also of all Germany; since no nation anywhere in the world except ourselves can show so old a true poetic association, never interrupted in several thousand (sic!) years, but at all times flourishing with the favor and privileges accorded it by the government, and with its own rules and regulations."

We may quote also a view which has the advantage of greater historical perspective, and is still just and appreciative:

„Ich will hier nicht den Unsinn der vielen Dichtergesellschaften herbeiziehen und strafen, aber die Meistersänger damit entschuldigen, dass, nachdem schon alle ihre Regel aus den wahren Schranken getreten war, die blösse Förmlichkeit auf die Reinheit ihrer Sitten gewirkt hat und ein Band gestiftet hat, werther denn ihre Kunst war. Der Meistergesang zeigt sich weithin als ein Mittel mehr, welches auf den Bund der Bürger wohlthätig gewirkt hat. ... Man ist leicht damit fertig gewesen, die Geschmacklosigkeit und Trockenheit der späteren Meistersänger zu tadeln, hat aber dabei die Ehrlichkeit und Selbstverkennung ganz übersehen, womit sie ihre fromme Kunst übten." [1])

---

1) Grimm: „Ueber den altdeutschen Meistergesang", 11.

CHAPTER I.
THE SOURCE FOR THE TECHNICAL DETAILS IN THE „MASTERSINGERS".

I. GENERAL CUSTOMS AND USAGES OF THE MASTERSINGERS IN THE SCHOOL AND AT THE REVEL.

The most detailed account of the observances of the Mastersingers in their public functions is to be found in Wagenseil's sixth chapter,[1]) a source closely followed by Wagner.

„In Nuremberg the Mastersingers are permitted to hold their Singing-schools on the afternoon of Sunday and of holidays as often as they like. ... And for this purpose has been thrown open from the earliest times the so-called Church of St. Catharine, perhaps because the same holy virgin and martyr was held to be a patron of the liberal arts et omnis elegantioris literæ in the Roman church, according to the manner in which Minerva was esteemed by the pagans."

Wagner, following this account, represents the School as having been held in this church. This is an anachronism for the time in which the „Mastersingers" is supposed to play, i. e. the middle of the sixteenth century, for it was not until the seventeenth century that the place of meeting was changed from the Church of St. Martha to that of St. Catharine.[2])

---

1) Wagenseil, 540 ff. All quotations not otherwise accredited are to be referred to this chapter passim.

2) See Ranisch: „Lebensbeschreibung Hanns Sachsen", 27 note, who gives a song written by one Wolf Bautner in 1620 which confirms this statement:
„Weil wir nun gar ein lange Zeit
Sind bey Sanct Marte gwesen,

„Several days before a Singing-school is to be held, the Markers or Directors of the Mastersingers Guild give notice of it, and such notice is given by the youngest Master, who shall go to the house of each Guildsman, nor shall he claim for this any recompense."

Compare Wagner (VII, 168):[1]
„Zu einer Freiung und Zunftberathung
ging an die Meister ein' Einladung."

Further:
„Every member of the guild who is summoned to the Singing-school is bound to appear, or if he cannot come, to have himself excused by a substitute."

Compare Wagner (VII, 169). In the roll-call, when Kothner comes to the name of Niklaus Vogel, who is absent, he is excused by his apprentice.

„In the midst of the church of St. Catharine, at the beginning of the choir, a low platform is erected, on which is set a table with a great black desk, and around the table are set benches, and this platform, which is called the Marker's Seat (Gemerke) hat curtains drawn around it, so that one cannot see from without what goes on within. A cathedra, in the form of a pulpit, in which he who is about to sing a Mastersong seats himself, remains always unchanged in its place, not far from the large pulpit in which the sermons are preached."

To this account correspond closely the stage-directions for this scene in Wagner (VII, 165).

„When the day appointed for the Singing-school has arrived, the advertisement of it is given by four or five tablets publicly hung up in the city, of which three are attached to the different

---

Und man dieselb Kirch gmeiner Stadt
Zu besserm Nutz thät wenden,
So hat ein hohe Obrigkeit
Uns die Kirch erlesen
St. Catharina an dem Ort,
Unser Gesang zu vollenden."

[1] These references in parenthesis are to Wagner: „Gesammelte Schriften und Dichtungen", 2nd ed., and are inserted in the text in order to facilitate reference.

stories of the great Market, the fourth however to the outer door[1]) through which one enters the church of St. Catharine."

The first tablet had on it a picture of the Rosegarden, the second „King David, depicted as playing on a harp as he kneels before the Lord Christ hanging on the cross" (a naïve anachronism!), the third the birth of Christ, the fourth the likeness of „honest Hans Sachs". To each tablet was added a printed bill of the following purport:

„In the Singing-school of today several
Lovers of the Art propose to the Mastersingers several prizes for Singing.
Therefore shall be sung first in the Open
Singing true and demonstrable Histories, edifying for Christendom.
The limit shall be from ... to ... ⎫
For the competition[2]) from ... to ... ⎬ Rimes
on the Principal Singing, no song shall be passed, unless it is in accordance with Holy Writ, i. e. from the Old and New Testament.
The limit shall be from ... to ... ⎫
For the competition from ... to ... ⎬ Rimes.
Let him who wishes to hear betake himself after mid-day service to St. Catharine's, where it will begin.

Sometimes the poster reads thus:

„Since by the favor of the Most Noble, Considerate and Wise Council of this city it is allowed and granted to the Mastersingers to call a public Christian Singing-school, and to hold it to the praise, honor and glory of God Almighty as also for the dissemination of his holy Divine Word, on this account in the aforesaid school shall be sung nothing except what is in accordance with holy Divine Writ; also it is forbidden to sing all abusive and irritating songs (Straffer und Reitzer) from which all discord springs, as well as all obscene songs. But he

---

1) The church of St. Catharine, once part of a monastery, is situated in a court, which is entered by a large gate. It is probably this court-gate, which opens on the street, that is here meant.

2) Das Gleichen. — This was the competitive singing for the prizes.

who with true art does the best shall be honored with the David or School-jewel, and the one second to him with a fair wreath."

The gathering of the audience in the church of St. Catharine occurs after the mid-day service, or an hour before vespers, according to the Nuremberg reckoning, that is at one o'clock." [1])

This fact gives Wagner a chance for the striking opening of his drama. The church-service is just ending, and we hear one stanza of what might be an old German hymn just as the curtain rises.

When a goodly number of people were present the Open Singing began, in which all, even strangers, might participate. In this exercise the subject might be „a true and honorable secular event" as well as something from the Bible. But in the Open Singing there was no marking, so that, beyond fame, one could win nothing, sing as one might.

„He who now wishes to sing, seats himself with fine courtesy in the singer's seat, takes off his hat or cap, and after he has paused for a while begins to sing and continues to the end." It will be seen from this that Walther commits a grave offense by rising from his seat in the excitement of his song (VII, 183).[2])

After the Open Singing came the Principal Singing (Haupt-Singen) in which might be sung only songs whose subjects came from the Bible. The singer was required to cite at the beginning of his song the book and chapter from which the subject was taken.

„When, in the Principal Singing, the singer has mounted the singing-seat and rested a while the chief Marker cries: Begin! Then the singer makes a beginning, and when a stanza or refrain is complete he stops until the Marker cries again: Go on! After the song is ended the singer betakes himself from his seat and gives place to another."

---

1) Time was ordinarily reckoned in Nuremberg according to the Italian or old Roman method.

2) See „Strassburger Studien", III, 206. There is a specific name for this, i. e. Stuelsprüngl, in the Ulm Register.

These two expressions are the „Fanget an!" [1]) and „Fahret fort!" [2]) which occur so often in Wagner.

The Markers, the most eminent men in the guild, criticized the songs. There were four of them, according to Wagenseil.[3]) The oldest, with Luther's version of the Bible before him, noticed whether the song agreed with the scriptural version, as well as whether it was couched in Luther's vocabulary. The second noticed the text, and marked down with chalk on the desk the errors against the Tablature. The third wrote down the riming words, and noted any errors in rime or in the verse-scheme, and the fourth criticized the melody.

„During the Singing the remaining Guildmembers must refrain from speaking or noise, that the singers may not become confused", says Wagenseil, an injunction not observed by the Masters as Walther proceeds with his trial-song (VII, 187 ff.). If there was a tie in the singing, those who had sung equally well were obliged to continue until one had sung entirely without mistakes (glatt gesungen) or at all events with fewer than the other.

There were two prizes, which were not, however, given outright, but only to be worn during the assembly and the following Revel. The first was a silver chain, hung with all sorts of medallions which had been presented to the society, the second a wreath of silk flowers. The chain was itself too cumbersome to wear, so a lighter one, hung with three silver and gilded medallions, was provided for the winner. This ornament received the name of the King David, for on the central medallion was a picture of King David playing on the harp, „and this Hans Sachs bequeathed to the company".[4]) The winner of the King David was privileged to sit at the next meeting with the Markers,

---

1) Wagner, VII, 159, 182, 218, 219, 263.
2) Ibid. VII, 220, 221, 267, 268.
3) Puschman, 30 gives three as the number. No Tablature gives less than two, and three seems to have been the usual number.
4) Wagenseil, 545. Wagenseil tells us with honest pride that he himself replaced this, since it had grown old, by a silver chain and a gilded medallion.

and remind them of their oversights, while the winner of the wreath stood at the door at the time of the next meeting and received the money.

Wagner deviates from this account in the disposal of the prizes. He makes the wreath the first prize, by virtue of which Walther wins Eva for his bride.

The apprentices announce this in the first act (VII, 165):
„Das Blumenkränzlein aus Seiden fein,
wird das dem Herrn Ritter beschieden sein?"

In the last act, after Walther's song is succesfully finished, Eva places on his brow a wreath" twined of laurel and myrtle" (VII, 269), (evidently Wagner thought this more auspicious than a silken wreath for the happy occasion); and the King David, a golden chain (not silver as in Wagenseil), with three medallions, is given him only to signify his elevation to the dignity of Mastersinger. Now in Wagenseil the King David is the first prize, the wreath the second, but what matters this when the artist's purposes are better served by a reversal of order?

The text of a song in one melody was open for a prize only once a year; but if the same text were adapted to a different melody it might be sung and rewarded several times. Two songs with the same melody were not to be sung the one immediately after the other. The Markers are adjured to mark truly and diligently, according to the intention of the art, and not according to bias . . . „not otherwise than as if one were sworn to it, although in truth one neither can nor ought to swear":[1] In case some relative of a Marker was to sing, the latter was required to resign his office for the time being to some unprejudiced person. Compare with this Sachs' utterance in the first act (VII, 186):
„Der Merker werde so bestellt,
dass weder Hass noch Lieben
das Urtheil trüben, das er fällt"

It rested with the judgment of the Marker whether the singer's errors

---

[1] Wagenseil, 545 f. This, as other passages, is taken directly from Puschman.

should be told him at once, or after the school in private, "that others may not scoff at him".¹)

As to how the uninitiated learned Mastersong and were taken into the Guild, we learn the following:

"If a person has desire and love for the Mastersingers art, he betakes himself to any Master in whom he has confidence and who has worn the jewel at least once, and begs him to assist him with good instruction. He who is thus besought will do so gladly, and undertakes the great labor which the teaching of such very difficult tunes entails entirely gratis, merely from a desire to further the art for posterity. On which account the Masters themselves seek for pupils, and for this cut short their rest and slep: since they must employ their day in the exercise of their trade and in the winning of food."

When an apprentice had learned the rules and a number of Melodies, including the four crowned Melodies,²) he was presented to the masters in the Revel (usually on St. Thomas' Day) for their acceptance. The Marker examined the candidate, asking whether he was of honorable birth, of a frivolous or quiet character, whether he visited the Singing-school regularly. He was further tested as to whether be had sufficient knowledge of the art, and knew what a vowel or consonant was, whether he knew the qualities of rimes, what were masculine and what femine, whether he knew a sufficient number of tunes, especially the four crowned tunes, and in case of necessity could mark a song. Compare Wagner (VII, 160):

"hab' ich das Leder glatt geschlagen,
lern' ich Vocal und Consonanz sagen;
wichst' ich den Draht gar fein und steif,
was sich da reimt, ich wohl begreif';

---

1) Hans Sachs suggests the following day as an appropriate time. See Genée, 412. „Item die mercker sint schuldig almal den nechsten tag nach der Singschuel seinen iden Singer der nit ze gleichen ist kumen, seinen fel so ers pegert an ze zaigen."

2) These were the Long Measures or Tunes of Heinrich Mügling, Heinrich Frauenlob, Ludwig Marner and Bartel Regenbogen respectively. Wagenseil, 354 ff.

>   den Pfriemen schwingend,
>   im Stich die Ahl',
>   was stumpf, was klingend"...

He was then given an opportunity to sing a Mastersong, and if he erred to the extent of more than seven mistakes, he could not be taken in. This is a condition twice repeated by **Wagner** (VII, 165, 181):

>   "Sieben Fehler giebt er euch vor,
>   die merkt er mit Kreide dort an,
>   wer über sieben Fehler verlor,
>   hat versungen und ganz verthan!"

After this the **Commendator** and **Candidatus** retired, and the oldest Marker enquired whether the candidate were agreeable to the company, and sufficiently skilled. If the answer was favorable the candidate must pledge himself:

I. To remain faithful to the art of song.

II. To defend the art and the Guild whenever he heard them attacked.

III. To live peaceably with his brother-members of the Guild, and to assist them where it was in his power, both in their bodily wants and in their reputations.

IV. To sing no Mastersong in the open streets by day or by night, nor at carouses or in unseemly places. Yet to a stranger inspired by a worthy desire to hear a Mastersong he should not refuse to sing one.

The older custom was then to baptize the novice with water, and by this ceremony the Apprentice (Lehrling) became a Singer. When the Singer became sufficiently skilled he was permitted to take part in the Open Singing, and was there announced as free (freigesprochen) and declared a Master. This is Wagner's „losgesprochen" (VII, 156):

>   "der Lehrling wird da losgesprochen,
>   der nichts wider die Tabulatur verbrochen;
>   Meister wird, wen die Prob' nicht reu't."

A Nuremberg Mastersinger, M. Ambrosius Metzger, gives a poetic account of the whole ceremony in the melodies of various Masters, a song which was in high repute in **Wagenseil**'s day.

No doubt the name of Apprentice, as well as many of the ceremonies of his reception as a Master, were borrowed from the usages of the trades-guilds.

After the Singing-school an „honorable, decorous and peaceful revel" was held in a neighboring tavern. All weapons were to be laid aside, play, useless conversation, superabundant drinking, were forbidden. A wreath was offered, for which anyone might sing. Irritating songs were forbidden, as provoking discord, and no one might challenge another to sing for money. No one might sit at table with the Markers unless expressly invited. The winner of the wreath in the Singing-school waited on the revel, and, if he needed aid, the winner of the wreath the previous time assisted. The wreath-winner and the Markers received a slight compensation for their services. The revel was paid for from the common funds of the guild.

Finally, a deceased Mastersinger was to be accompanied to the grave by all the members of the guild, and when a Marker died, a song was to be sung by them all in his honor at the grave.

II. THE TABLATURE.

The rules of the Mastersingers' School were drawn up in the so-called Tablature, a code defining the errors which might be committed, and prescribing the punishment for each. The oldest Tablature preserved is that of the Nuremberg School, of the year 1540. The one followed by Wagner is again that contained in Wagenseil, who here follows Puschman closely, but in a different order. First come a few general definitions.[1])

A **Bar** is, accordig to Wagenseil, a complete poem, not as Wagner uses it (VII, 240), a single stanza. Each Bar has its regular rime-and verse-structure, ordained and preserved by the lips of the Master. „This all the Singers, Poets and Markers should know how to measure and count off on their fingers",

---

1) Wagenseil, 521 ff. All technical words used by Wagner which are taken from this chapter of Wagenseil will be designated by being printed in capitals.

says our authority. A Bar is composed of several Stanzas (**Gesätze**).

A Stanza is composed of Strophe and Antistrophe (**Stollen**), which are identical in metrical and melodic structure, and a Refrain (**Abgesang**) of different organization.[1]) The Refrain is some times followed by another strophe.

How exactly Wagner has turned the very language of Wagenseil into his verse may be seen from the following passages from each:[2])

Wagenseil:	Wagner:
„Ein jedes Meister-Gesangs Bar hat sein ordentlich Gemäs, in Reimen und Silben ...	„Ein jedes Meistergesanges Bar stell' ordentlich ein Gemässe dar
Ein Bar hat mehrentheils unterschiedliche Gesätz oder Stuck, als viel deren der Tichter tichten mag.	aus unterschiedlichen Gesetzen, < die Keiner soll verletzen.
Ein Gesätz bestehet meistentheils aus zweyen Stollen, die gleiche Melodey haben.	Ein Gesetz bestehet aus zweenen Stollen, die gleiche Melodei haben sollen,
Ein Stoll bestehet aus etlichen Versen ...	der Stoll' aus etlicher Vers' Gebänd', der Vers hat seinen Reim am End'.
Darauf folgt das Abgesang so auch etliche Vers begreifft, welches aber eine besondere und andere Melodey hat als die Stollen."	Darauf so folgt der Abgesang, der sei auch etlich' Verse lang, und hab' sein' besondere Melodei, als nicht im Stollen zu finden sei."

Then follow six classes of rime, given by Puschman also.[3])

---

1) The Mastersingers compared their verses with an architectural structure. The **Stollen** are the two upright beams and the **Abgesang** is the cross-beam laid upon them. The same structure existed in Minnesong, and is the fundamental principle of the sonnet and the sonata. See Walther von der Vogelweide, herausg. v. Pfeiffer, 5.

2) cf. „Nord und Süd", LXXII, 238. Wagenseil, 521 f. Wagner, VII, 241 f.

3) Puschman, 7.

I. Masculine rimes are called Dull Rimes (**Stumpfe Reime**), II. feminine are called Resonant Rimes (**Klingende Reime**). Compare Wagner (VII, 160) „was stumpf, was klingend".

III. Orphans (**Waisen**, VII, 161) are end-words of a verse which rime with nothing else, either in their own or in a following verse. They may occur in the middle of a verse, or, as is more usual, at the end.

IV Germ-rimes (**Körner**), are words riming with nothing else in their own stanza, but which have a rime corresponding to them in each following stanza.

V Pauses (**Pausen**) are monosyllables at the beginning, end, or sometimes middle of a stanza, which stand alone as an entire verse, riming however with one another. Compare Wagner (VII, 161):

„was Pausen, was Körner."

VI Beat-rimes (**Schlag-Reime**, VII, 164), are verses consisting of one trochaic or iambic foot.

No single verse may have more than thirteen syllables, since one cannot sing more in a single breath, especially if there are any runs or flourishes.[1]). Compare Wagner (VII, 162):

„mit dem Athem spart, dass er nicht knappt,
und gar am End' ihr überschnappt."

Following this category is a list of thirty-three mistakes with their penalties. The mistakes were counted by syllables, and each singer was permitted to make seven before he had outsung himself (**Versungen**, VII, 162). Puschman enumerates thirty-two errors, and divides them into two classes, 1. the mistakes which must always be marked, and 2. those which are to be marked only when the superiority of one singer cannot be decided by the ordinary marking.[2]) There are twenty-three mistakes in his first category, and eleven in his second. Wagenseil makes no such distinction, and his order is this.[3]) —

---

1) cf. Puschman, 9.
2) Ibid. 10 ff. This was called marking rigorously („in die Schärfe".)
3) The Roman numerals in parenthesis give Puschman's numbering for his first category, the Arabic that for his second.

(I) I. A Fault against the noble German Language. — The language of Luther's Bible ¹) and of the Chanceries was the norm, and the only deviation allowed from this was in the case of strangers, who might use their own dialect, provided they did so consistently. For instance a Nuremberger might sing: „Er ist ein frommer Mon" to go with „Er ist auf rechter Bon", but not to go with „Und er ging davon."

(II) II. False Opinions are „all false, superstitious, visionary, unchristian and unseemly doctrines, stories, anecdotes and shameless and wanton words, which run counter to the pure, blessed doctrine of Jesus Christ, to good life, good morals, good conduct, and integrity.²) Anyone guilty of this fault was outsung, and might even be expelled from the school.

(III) III. Bad Latin is all Latin sung contra Grammaticæ leges incongrue. Mastersingers who have not studied this language are to have their Latin corrected by a Latin scholar. This fault included mistakes in quantity, and was marked syllable for syllable.

(IV) IV. A Blind Meaning (**Blinde Meinung**, VII, 184) is an incomplete or unclear expression, as, „Ich, du sol kommen" for „Ich und du sol kommen." This is also marked syllable for syllable.

(V) V. A Blind Word is a word which is not clear or easily unterstood, as „Sag" for „Sach", a tenuis for an aspirate. A blind word takes off two syllables. This is probably what Beckmesser means when be accuses Walther of „unklare Wort'" (VII, 188).

(VI) VI. A Half-Word is the shortening of a word by one syllable, apocope, as: „Ich kan es dir nit sag" for „sagen". The forfeit was two syllables.

(VII) VII. An Offense (**Laster**, VII, 187) is the change of a vowel in a word for the sake of the rime, as „Sohn: Mon."

---

1) This statement occurs only in Puschman and Wagenseil. It was hardly a universal regulation of the schools, and certainly not until a late period. See Pietsch: „Martin Luther und die hochdeutsche Schriftsprache", 89 ff.

2) Wagenseil, 525.

The forfeit for this was two syllables. "Laster" is an ambiguous expression, denoting different errors in different schools. Sometimes it was applied to verses two or more of which began with the same word or words. Still others considered it a "Laster" to have assonant words follow each other. It is clearly a translation of the Latin vitium, taken from the schools.[1])

(1) VIII. An Addition (Anhang) is the making of a monosyllable dissyllabic on account of the exigencies of the rime, as "Es ist ein frommer Mane" for "Mann". This was punished by half a syllable. Puschman[2]) glosses it by its technical name, Paragoge, and makes the forfeit one syllable.

(6) IX. A Contracted Syllable (Klebsilbe, VII, 161) is, as its name implies, the contraction of two syllables into one, as "keim" for "keinem". The forfeit was half a syllable. Puschman gives it as one syllable.[3])

(8) X. A Relative (Relativum) is a word governing two clauses. The example cited is "Was nit recht gesungen wird gestrafft" for "Was nit recht gesungen wird, wird gestrafft". This is noted only if one desires to be hypercritical in song.

(4) XI. A Difference (Differenz, VII, 188) is the reversal of the vowels of a diphthong, as "Deib" for "Dieb". Puschman however regards this as a venial error[4]) and the marking of it as hair-splitting ("klügeln"). This was punished by three syllables. Others regarded a Difference as the unnecessary repetition of a word, as "Der Herr der sprach".

(9) XII. Adjacent words (Anrührende Wörter) is the beginning of one verse with the word which ends the preceding, as:

"Wer Hader macht
Macht sich veracht."

Wagenseil, as well as Puschman, relegates this into the category of mistakes which were not usually marked.

---

1) See "Strassburger Studien", III, 204 f.
2) Puschman, 17, 11.
3) Ibid. 12.
4) Ibid. 19.

XIII. An Unrhetorical (**Unredbar**, VII, 187) Phrase is one in which the order of words is different from that in spoken language. In estimating errors it was counted as one syllable. The example is:

„Der Vater mein
Ist fromm und fein
Die Mutter gut
Mir gütlich thut."

I am inclined to think that this article was put in under the influence of Opitz' „Buch von der Deutschen Poeterey", Wagenseil had great regard for him, calling him „der mit einem unverwelcklichen Lorbeerkranz Gekrönte Martin Opitz".[1] This article is not in Puschman, nor in the Nuremberg or Colmar Tablatures. It is interesting to notice that, in spite of the dictum of Opitz,[1] the Middle High German construction, common in the Folksong, has gained the day, and is no longer „unrhetorical".

(VIII) XIV. Equivocal Words (**Aequivoca**, VII, 188) are words spelled alike, but with different meanings, as „Stecken" a staff, and „stecken", to be fast. This fault forfeits four syllables.

(IX) XV. A Half-Equivocum (Halb-Aequivocum) is the partial coincidence of a feminine and masculine rime, as for example:

„Sie geben, was sie haben,
Ich auch das, was ich hab" u. s. w.

Thir error forfeits two syllables.

XVI. Accumulated Equivoca (Ueberhoff[2] Aequivoca) is the repetition of two or more rimes of one strophe in another part of the same song. The forfeit for this is three syllables.

(X) XVII. A False Scheme (**Falsch Gebänd**, VII, 187) is a variation in versification from the scheme of the original Mastersong. The forfeit is two syllables.

---

[1] Opitz: „Buch von der Deutschen Poeterey", reprint in „Neudrucke deutscher Litteraturwerke des XVI und XVII Jahrhunderts", 30.

[2] „Ueberhoff" = „überhäuft". It occurs in the form „überhauf" in Behaim. See „Germania", III, 310.

(XII) XVII. Isolated Rime (Blosse Reime) are verses left unrimed which ought to be rimed according to the scheme of versification. The forfeit is four syllables.

(XIII) XIX. Hesitation (Stutzen oder Zucken) is a pause at the wrong place, caused by carelessness or forgetfulness. As many syllables are forfeited as might be pronounced in the duration of the pause.

(XIV) XX. Mites (Milben, VII, 161) are words apocopated for the sake of the rime, as:

„Von diesem Dinge
Will ich jetzo singe."

The forfeit is one syllable.[1])

(XIII) XXI. Two Verses in one Breath (Zween Reimen oder Verss in einem Athem) explains itself. The end of each verse was marked by a pause and a new breath, hence he who failed to pause shortened the stanza by one verse. The forfeit was four syllables. This is Wagner's „falscher Athem" (VII, 188).

(XV) XXII. Too Short and too Long (Zu Kurtz und zu Lang, VII, 161) was the mistake of putting less or more syllables in a verse than its master had done. The forfeit was as many syllables as there were in the error made.

(XVI) XXIII. Repetition (Hinter sich und fur sich litterally „back or forward") is 1. going back to repeat something that has been left out, 2. the repetition of what has been already sung, in order to be think onesself of the following verse, 3. the repetition of one or more words already sung, through carelessness. This error forfeits syllable for syllable.

(XVII) XXIV. Soft and Hard (Lind und Hart, VII, 160) is the riming of two words, of which one ends in a voiced, the other in an unvoiced consonant, or the one in a double, the other in a single consonant; for example, Laden: Thaten, Gott: Tod. This error forfeited syllable for syllable.

(XVIII) XXV. Too High or too Low (Zu Hoch und zu Niedrig, VII, 162) is pitching a tune so high or so low that the

---

1) „Milben" refers to a slight error, which is to be compænd in its insignificance to a mite. cf. „Strassburger Studien", III, 217 and Mey, 29.

singer cannot complete it in the same key. This error forfeits six syllables (in Puschman only one![1]) This is Wagner's „zu hoch, zu tief".

(XIX) XXVI. Singing and Speaking (Singen und Reden). This error was committed when the singer interrupted his song by speaking without being spoken to, and the forfeit was as many syllables as were in the interpolated speech.

(XX) XXVII. Change of Melody (**Veränderung der Thön**) might be a change from stanza to stanza, or a change within the stanza from the number of verses in the original form. For every verse changed the forfeit was four syllables. This is perhaps David's „Verwechseltet ihr" (VII, 162).

(XXI) XXVIII. False Melody (**Falsche Melodey**) is an absolute change of the entire measure. One who commits such an error is entirely outsung. Puschman, however, gives as the forfeit for this only two syllables. Compare Wagner's „verkehrt, verstellt der ganze Bar" (VII, 188).

XXIX. [Here by oversight Wagenseil repeats essentially No. XVII.]

(XXII) XXX. False Flourishes or Coloratures (**Falsche Blumen oder Coloratur**) are runs and ornamental notes put in by the singer which do not occur in the original song. These, if short, forfeit one syllable, if long, two. Compare for this Wagner (VII, 162):

„nicht ändert an „Blum" und „Coloratur",
jed' Zierath fest nach des Meisters Spur."

(XXIII) XXXI. A Change of Song (**Auswechsslung der Lieder**) is the singing of a different number of stanzas than was in the original song. This forfeits as many syllables as there were in the stanzas added or omitted.[2]) Compare for this Wagner (VII, 162), „verwechselt ihr".

XXXII. Resonance before or after (**Vor- und Nach-Klang**). This was humming with closed lips before or after a song, either

---

1) How rudimentary was the knowledge of music among these worthies, when such rules were necessary!

2) Since only seven syllables were allowed to go forfeit, anyone who erred in this point must be entirely outsung.

of which errors forfeited one syllable. This is also incorporated in David's instructions to the young knight (VII, 162):
„Vor dem Wort mit der Stimme ja nicht summt,
Nach dem Wort mit dem Mund ja nicht brummt."
(XXIV) XXXIII. Becoming Confused (Irren oder Irr Werden, VII, 162) is erring in text, melody, rime, or any or all parts of a stanza. He who commits this fault is quite outsung, „for it is to be noted that all Mastersongs are to be sung out of one's head, and never out of a book".[1])

Following this formal category of rules are some general remarks about the melodies or tunes.[2])

„Every Mastersinger shall be zealous to sing plain good German slowly and modestly, and to every verse must be given its appropiate pause, and two or three verses must not be shouted out in one breath ...

It is called singing smoothly (glatt singen) when nothing can be criticized in the singing."

No Master-tune might infringe on another to the extent of more than four syllables; both melody and coloratures must be entirely new. Thus we read in Wagner (VII, 181):
„wer ein neues Lied gericht',
das über vier der Silben nicht
eingreift in and'rer Meister Weis',
dess' Lied erwerb' sich Meister-Preis."
The new Tune was ordinarily sung by the Master himself three times before the entire School, first, as low as possible, then in the ordinary pitch in which it would be sung in the school, and finally pitched as high as possible. If the Mastersinger himself were too old to sing it, another might sing it for him, provided he sat by and vouched for it as his own. If the Tune were approved it was given „an honorable and not a contemptuous name", and had two god-fathers chosen, a ceremony taken from the trades-guilds. This ceremony Wagner introduces in a modified form in the third act (VII, 254 ff.), where Hans Sachs christens

---

1) Wagenseil, 531.
2) Ibid. 532.

Walther's Morningdream-measure. After this the inventor of the tune was to compose three stanzas to it on a subject assigned by the Markers, and the tune was then written down in the Mastersingers' book, with the name of the composer. Singers in places where there were no Schools might sing their tunes and have them recorded in cities where Schools existed.

Since none of the twelve old Masters made stanzas with less than seven verses, no tune with stanzas of lesser length were admitted — „yet the Short Measure of Heinrich Mügling is said to have only five verses".[1]) The maximum limit Wagenseil puts at one hundred verses, not that longer stanzas were not allowed, but that in marking they had no preference over shorter ones. Among the older Masters they had not been so long as in later times, he tells us. The four crowned Tunes had the preference, and one was permitted an extra syllable for forfeit in each stanza, „for the sake of the twelve old Masters, through whom the art first came to light".[2])

At stated times the Tablature was read before the Revel, and obscure points were explained by the Markers.

Finally we have a definition of the different ranks of the society. He who did not understand everything in the Tablature was called a Pupil (Schüler), he who understood it all a School-friend (Schulfreund). He who could sing five or six Tunes was a Singer, he who could make songs to the Tunes of others was a Poet (Dichter), and he who invented a Tune was a Master. But all who were enrolled in the society were called Associates (Gesellschafter). This corresponds to the explanation by David in the first act of these various terms (VII, 159 ff.).

While the greater part of these technical terms are thus to be found in Wagenseil, there still remain three which occur neither here, nor in any book on Mastersong to which I have

---

1) Wagenseil, 533.
2) Ibid. 533. cf. Puschman, 29, who gives these Tunes no preference. In Mayence for a long period no Tunes might be sung except these four. See Sachs: „Dichtungen", in „Deutsche Dichter des sechszehnten Jahrhunderts", IV, „Einleitung", XIX.

had access. These terms are: "Flickgesang", "Schrollen" and "Überfall" (VII, 188). "Flickgesang" is perfectly comprehensible in itself, as being an interpolation in the regular verse-scheme. "Schrollen" may be Wagner's careless reading of "Schullende Reimen",¹) a kind of Laster. If we take it as it stands in Wagner, it is capable of interpretation as meaning "uncouth" or "clumsy" rhymes.²) "Überfall" occurs in no dictionary, musical or otherwise, so for as I have been able to find out. I am reluctantly compelled to attribute these words, since they are in quotation-marks, to an as yet unknown source. "Dörner" (VII, 161) is another term which does not occur in the Tablature, but is introduced by analogy, or for the sake of the rhyme. If there are "Blumen" in Mastersong, why not "Dörner" also, reasons David.

III. THE MASTERSINGERS TUNES.

The entire list of Mastersingers Tunes, so glibly enumerated by David³) is also in Wagenseil in his list of "Meister-Thöne, welche dieser Zeit, und sonderlich zu Nurnberg, pflegen gesungen zu werden".⁴) I give them in Wagner's order.

Name of Tune		Author	No. of verses
Short Tune	Der kurze Ton	Barthel Regenbogen	7
		Michael Francke	7
		Conrad Nachtigal	7
		Severin Kriegsauer	7
		Cantzler	11
		Nunnebeck	11
		Hans Sachs	13

1) Wagenseil, 526.
2) Sanders: "Worterbuch", II, 1015, article "Schroll".
3) Wagner, VII, 161 f.
4) Wagenseil, 534 ff.

Name of Tune		Author	No. of verses
Long Tune	Der lange Ton	Hans Vogel	14
		Heinrich Mügling	20
		Hopfengarten	20
		Regenbogen	23
		Frauenlob	24
		Ludwig Marner	27
		Caspar Singer	29
Overlong Tune [1])			
Writing-paper Measure	Die Schreibpapier-Weise	M. Ambrosius Metzger	10
Black-ink Measure	Die Schwarz-Dinten-Weise		9
Red Tune	Der rothe Ton	Peter Zwinger	15
Blue Tune	Der blaue Ton	Regenbogen	16
		Frauenlob	17
Green Tune [2])			
Hedge-blossom Measure	Die Hageblüh-Weise	Frauenlob	9
Grass-blade Measure	Die Strohhalm-Weise	M. Ambrosius Metzger	9
Fennel Measure	Die Fengel-Weise	Hans Findeisen	9
Tender Tune	Der zarte Ton	Frauenlob	21
Sweet Tune	Der süsse Ton	Georg Schüller	18
Rose-tone Measure	Die Rosenthon-Weise	Hans Sachs	20
Short-love Tune	Der kurzen Liebe Ton	Michael Vogel	12

1) Of Overlong Tunes there are none in Wagenseils list, but Wagner may have formed this by analogy with the Overshort Tnne of Georg Hager, and the Overtender Tune of Frauenlob. Overlong Tunes do, however, occur in other lists of Mastersongs. Hans Sachs was the inventor of one with sixty-three rimes. See Ranisch, 132.

2) The Green Tune does not occur in this list alone, but there is a Green-vinegard Measure, and a Greelinden-blossom Measure, from which this may be taken.

Name of Tune		Author	No. of verses
Forgotten Tune	Der vergessene Ton	Frauenlob	15
Rosemary Measure	Die Rosmarin-Weise	Hans Friedlein	8
Yellow-violet Measure	Die Gelbveiglein-Weise	M. Ambrosius Metzger	13
Rainbow Measure [1])			
Nightingale Measure [2])			
English-tin Measure	Die englische Zinnweise	Kaspar Enderles	21
Cinnamon-stick Measure	Die Zimmtröhren-Weise	M. Ambrosius Metzger	27
Fresh-pomegranate Measure	Die frische Pomeranzen-Weise [2])		28
Green-linden-blossom Measure	Die grüne Lindenblüh-Weise	Beschreier	30
Frog Measure	Die Frösch-Weise	Frauenlob	18
Calves Measure	Die Kälber-Weise	Heiden	20
Thistle-finch Measure	Die Stieglitz-Weise	Adam Puschman	15
Deceased-glutton Measure	Die abgeschiedene Vielfrass-Weise	Carl Foder	12
Lark Measure	Die Lerchen-Weise	Heinrich Ender	22
Barkers Tune	Der Beller-Ton	Severin Kriegsauer	22
Snail Measure	Die Schnecken-Weise	M. Ambrosius Metzger	7
Balsam-blossom Measure	Die Melissenblümlein-Weise	.	17
(Sweet-smelling-) majorem Measure	(Die wohlriechend-) Meiran-Weise	.	20

1) There are no Rainbow and Nightingale Tunes, but there are Tunes by authors of these names.
2) The author's name is not given.

Name of Tune		Author	No. of verses
Yellow-lion-skin Measure	Die Gelblöwenhaut-Weise	M. Ambrosius Metzger	23
True-pelican Measure	Die treu Pelikan-Weise	„	18
Brightly-gleamingwise Measure [1])	Die buttglänzende Draht-Weise	Jobst Zolner	23

Later on, where Beckmesser is rating the errors of Walther's trial-song [2]) he mentions four more Tunes from this same list.

Adventure Measure	Die Abenteuer-Weise	Hans Folz	20
Blue-Lark-spur Measure	Die blau Rittersporn-Weise	M. Ambrosius Metzger	20
Lofty-pine-tree Measure	Die hoch Tannen-Weise	Heinrich Wolf	20
Proud youth Measure	Die stolz Jüngling-Weise	M. Ambrosius Metzger	20

The „Knieriem-Schlag-Weis'" and the „Eitel-Brodt- und Wasser Weis'",[3]) as well as the „Arm-Hunger-Weise",[4]) Wagner humourously makes up, but the „Harte-Tritt-Weis'" [5]) is in Wagenseil's list.

Heavy-tread Measure	Die harte Tritt-Weise	Daniel Steiglein	2

The „Schlag-reim" is taken from the Tablature.[6]) The name

---

1) A conjectural translation, reading „butt" as a misprint for „bunt". Bayard Taylor: „Studies in German Literature", 144 translates it „blood", reading „blut" here. Reading it as it is, it is quite capable of referring to the copper hoop with which the wooden buts, carried so often by the women of Bavaria, are hooped. These might „gleam brightly" in the sun.
2) Wagner, VII, 184.
3) Ibid. VII, 162.
4) Ibid. VII, 164.
5) Ibid. VII, 164.
6) Ibid. VII, 164.

given to Walther's prize-song, "die selige Morgentraumdeut-Weise" (VII, 255) is also a fine invention of Wagner's own. Wagner has chosen very skillfully from the two hundred and twenty-two Measures of Wagenseil's list just those which are most characteristic of the Mastersingers fanciful and oftentimes fantastic nomenclature, and to one who has studied Mastersong this is one of the most familiar touches. There is an artist's purpose in picking out just the best named Tunes by which the jealous Beckmesser may characterize the young knight's trial-song — "die Abenteuer-", "blau Rittersporn-", "hoch Tannen-", and "stolz Jüngling-Weise", all of which apply to the noble youth whom Beckmesser instinctively feels is above him.

IV. DRAMATIS PERSONÆ.

These are taken directly from Wagenseil[1]) who gives the list of the twelve old Nuremberg Mastersingers as follows: 1. Veit Pogner, 2. Cuntz Vogelsang, 3. Hermann Ortel, 4. Conrad Nachtigal, 5. Fritz Zorn, 6. Sixtus Beckmesser, 7. Fritz Kothner, 8. Niclaus Vogel, 9. Augustin Moser, 10. Hans Schwarz, 11. Ulrich Eisslinger, 12. Hans Folz. The same list is given in Schilter.[2])

The list of Nuremberg Masters was evidently a somewhat variable one, for Hans Sachs gives the following one:[3])

"1. Kunrat Nachtigall, ein peck. — 2. Fritz Zoren, ein nagler. — '3. Fogelgesang, heftelmacher. — 4. Herman Oertel, heftelmacher. — 5. Fritz Ketner. — 6. Mertin Grim. — 7. Sixt Peckmesser. — 8. vom Gosten-Hoff, ein schneider. — 9. Hans Schwartz, priefmaler. — 10. Ulrich Eislinger, holzmesser. — 11. Hans Foltze, balbirer. — 12. Lienhart Nunnenpeck, weber."

It will be seen that the list of Hans Sachs does not agree with that of Wagenseil, nor hence with that of Wagner. The occupation of most of the Masters is also given, but in no case

---

1) Wagenseil, 515.
2) "Thesaurus", III, 88.
3) Condensed from his Mastersong, "Ein Schulkunst". See his "Dichtungen", in "Deutsche Dichter des sechzehnten Jahrhunderts", IV, 102 ff.

does it correspond with that assigned by Wagner to his characters. Since Wagenseil does not mention the callings of the worthy Masters whose names he gives, we may conclude that Wagner made his list of callings from whole cloth.

Wagner likewise changes the name of Fritz Zorn to Balthazar Zorn, a change perhaps made for euphonic reasons. Fritz Zorn, with the two hard tz sounds coming together, would be difficult to sing, while Balthazar is not only more euphonious, but makes easier metre. The eighth in Wagenseil's list, Niclaus Vogel, while not given in the list of acting persons, exists in absentia, as it were, in the drama, for his name is called in the roll of Mastersingers in the first act (VII, 169 f.).

„Kothner.
Niklaus Vogel? — Schweigt?
Ein Lehrbube (sich schnell von der Bank erhebend)
Ist krank.
Kothner.
Gut' Bess'rung dem Meister!
Alle Meister.
Woll's Gott!
Der Lehrbube.
Schön Dank!"

Wagner has made a slight mistake in the name of Kothner. Following Wagenseil, who agrees with Schilter[1]) he spells it „Kothner". Puschman, however, and Hans Sachs[2]) in more than one place, have the name „Ketner", which is undoubtedly right. In Wagenseil's list of Mastersongs[3]) he has the name twice correctly written, „Fridrich Ketner". This is a good illustration of the fact that Wagner's comparison of sources was not wide.

There is a slight anachronism in bringing Hans Folz und Hans Sachs into the same play, for Hans Folz died before Hans Sachs began to compose, and was in fact one of the pioneers

---

1) Wagenseil, 515; Schilter, III. 89.
2) Puschman, 8; Genée, 461, 477.
3) Wagenseil, 535, 536.

of the art in Nuremberg. Genée says:[1] „Erst Hans Folz, dessen dichterische Thätigkeit in den Zeitraum von 1470—1490 fiel, scheint dem Meistergesang in Nürnberg grossen Aufschwung gegeben zu haben, und er kann wohl, nach der grossen Verehrung zu urtheilen, die er noch bei Hans Sachs genoss, als der eigentliche Begründer und Mittelpunct der älteren Nürnberger Singschule betrachtet werden."

Several of these Masters have Tunes ascribed to them in Wagenseil's list of Mastertunes.[2]

Hans Sachs is credited with ten Tunes[3] although he really wrote thirteen. The ten here cited are:

with 13 rimes: Der kurze Ton.
„ 20 „ Die Silberweise.
„ 20 „ Die Spruchweise.
„ 20 „ Die Rosentonweise.
„ 21 „ Der klingende Ton.
„ 22 „ Der goldene Ton.
„ 24 „ Der bewährte Ton.
„ 25 „ Der neue Ton.
„ 27 „ Die Morgenweise.
„ 34 „ Der schlechte lange Ton.

Hans (Kunz?) Vogelgesang has only one:
with 30 rimes: Der goldene Ton.

Five occur by Conrad Nachtigal:
with 5 rimes: Der kurze Ton.
„ 5 „ Die kurze Tagweise.
„ 9 „ Der sanfte Ton.
„ 23 „ Der schlechte lange Ton.
„ 25 „ Der Leidton.

„Der geschiedene Ton Nachtigals", with seventeen rimes, may also be his, although in every other case his full name is given.

---

[1] Genée, 254.
[2] Wagenseil, 534 ff.
[3] A complete list of his Tunes is given in his mss. „Generalregister" in the „Ratsbibliothek" at Zwickau. The remaining three are, „Die hohe Bergweise", „Die Gesangweise", „Der überlange Ton." See Genée, 464.

Friedrich Ketner has three Tunes:
> with 16 rimes: Die Osterweise.
> „ 22 „ Der Frauenton.
> „ 29 „ Der Barat-Reihen.

Fritz Zorn has also three Tunes:
> with 23 rimes: Der verhohlne Ton.
> „ 24 „ Der unbenannte Ton.
> „ 25 „ Die Zugweise.

Eislinger is credited with only one Tune:
> with 14 rimes: Die Maienweise.

as well as Hermann Oertel:
> with 34 rimes: Der Leidton.

Hans Folz is represented by seven Tunes:
> with 8 rimes: Der Theilton.
> „ 10 „ Die Feilweise.
> „ 18 „ Der Baumton.
> „ 20 „ Die Abenteuerweise.
> „ 21 „ Der hohe Ton.
> „ 28 „ Die Schrankweise.
> „ 30 „ Der freie Ton.

The other worthy Nuremberg Masters do not appear in Wagenseil's list of popular composers at all.[1]) There were two Vogels, Hans and Michael respectively, but no Niklaus. In the mss. „Generalregister" of Hans Sachs, in the section headed: „Hierauf folgen die thön der Nürnberger Dichter", we find the names of Fritz Ketner, Hermann Ortel, Vogelgesang, Hans Schwarz, Sixtus Beckmesser, Fritz Zorn, Cunrat Nachtigal, Hans Folz, Ulrich Eislinger, and Michael and Hans Vogel, but nowhere Niklaus.[2])

V. THE OCCURRENCE OF THE MASTERSINGERS STANZA IN WAGNER'S „MASTERSINGERS".

The occurrence of the Mastersingers stanza **(Gesätz)** in our music-drama is quite frequent. The first one which occurs is in

---

1) Wagenseil's list is, however, incomplete and faulty. See „Strass. Stud." III, 151.
2) Genée, 461.

the first part of Pogner's speech praising the art of Mastersong and offering Eva as a prize to the best singer (VII, 171 f.). The stanza begins: „Das schöne Fest, Johannistag", the antistrophe begins: „Die Singschul' ernst im Kirchenchor", the refrain begins: „Zu einem Werb'- und Wett-Gesang", and ends apparently ten lines below. The scheme is therefore as follows:[1])

	Strophe	Antistrophe	Refrain
1	4 m a (8)	4 m c (8)	4 m e (8)
2	3 f b (7)	3 f d (7)	3 f f (7)
3	4 m a (8)	4 m c (8)	4 m e (8)
4	4 m a (8)	4 m c (8)	3 f f (8)
5	3 f b (7)	3 f d (7)	4 m g (8)
6	3 f b (7)	3 f d (7)	4 m g (8)
7	4 m a (8)	4 m c (8)	3 f h (7)
8			3 f h (7)
9			3 m i (6)
10			3 m i (6)

Again, where Walther is answering the questions of Kothner in regard to his master in singing and where he learned the art, his replies make perfect strophe and antistrophe, as Vogelsang informs us (VII, 178 f.):

„Zwei art'ge Stollen fasst' er da ein."

Walther's answer to Kothner's next question forms the refrain. The scheme is as follows.

	Strophe	Antistrophe	Refrain
1	4 m a (8)	4 m a (8)	2 m b (4)
2	4 m a (8)	4 m a (8)	2 m b (4)
3	4 m b (8)	4 m b (8)	3 f e (7)
4	4 m b (8)	4 m b (8)	4 m b (8)
5	4 m b (8)	4 m b (8)	3 f e (7)
6	3 f c (7)	3 f d (7)	2 m f (4)

---

[1]) The first row of numerals designates the number of lines in each part, the first row under each heading is the number of accented syllables. The numerals in parenthesis give the entire number of syllables in the line. The other symbols are self-explanatory.

	Strophe	Antistrophe	Refrain
7	4 m a (8)	4 m a (8)	2 m f (4)
8	3 f e (8)	3 f d (7)	2 m g (4)
9			2 m g (4)
10			3 f h (7)
11			4 m i (8)
12			3 f h (7)
13			4 m i (8)
14			3 f j (7)
15			4 m i (8)
16			3 f j (7)

These will he perhaps enough stanzas to give in detail. Walther's trial-song (VII, 182 ff.), is one long stanza of eighty-one lines. The strophe and antistrophe are each twenty-nine hires long, the refrain twenty-three. The strophe begins: „Fanget an!" and ends: „Zu Schaden könnte bringen." The antistrophe begins: „Doch: fanget an!" and ends, not where Beckmesser interrupts, but after Walther continues his song, with „die Elstern, Kräh'n und Dohlen". The refrain comprises all the rest. Beckmesser's Serenade (VII, 219 ff.) in the second act, is an excellent travesty, not of Mastersong as it really was, but of it as it appears in Wagner. The serenade forms three stanzas, of which the strophes and antistrophes are each seven lines long, and the refrains six. The effect of the misplaced accents is irresistibly lucidrous, and quite in keeping with the genuine Mastersong, which went by count of syllables, not by accent.

Walther's „Selige Morgentraumdeut-Weise" is a Bar of three stanzas. The first two he makes under Sachs' direction, the third under the immediate inspiration of the presence of Eva in the work-shop. The three stanzas begin as follows:

I. „Morgenlich leuchtend in rosigem Schein" (VII, 239).
II. „Abendlich glühend in himmlischer Pracht" (VII, 241).
III. „Weilten die Sterne im lieblichen Tanz?" (VII, 251).

The Prize-song of Walther is, however, quite a different affair from this. It will be remembered that after Walther has sung the first strophe of the first stanza, the Masters let fall the paper which contains the Morning-song, and from here on

Walther allows himself great freedom, and makes the entire Bar into one long stanza, of which the strophe extends from „Morgenlich leuchtend" to „Eva im Paradies", the anti-strophe from „Abendlich dämmernd" to „die Muse des Parnass", and the refrain from here to „Parnass und Paradies" (VII, 267 ff.).

Mey[1]) not only points out these stanzas within the drama, but declares that the entire drama is, in its general content, one stupendous stanza, a curious comparison, and one which cannot be followed out too closely, although the first and second acts are in a measure counterparts, leading up to the third in conclusion.

VI. WAGNER'S GENERAL TREATMENT OF HIS MATERIAL.

Wagner has not hesitated to alter the historical basis of his drama to suit his needs. That, in spite of his not inconsiderable liberties, he has still succeeded in giving us the best and most vivid general historic impression of this peculiar organization and of the burgher-life of the time, redounds to his credit as a synthetic artist.

A regular School of the Mastersingers would have been impossible for Wagner's purposes, first, because he could not have introduced Walther's love-song, (since the subjects must all be Biblical in these sessions), and secondly, because only Mastersingers might take part in them, and Walther was not even an apprentice in the art. Wagner must introduce then the Open Singing, in which even strangers might participate, and in which the subjects might be secular. Hence David's explanation (VII, 156):

> „Nur Freiung heut';
> der Lehrling wird da losgesprochen,
> der nichts wider die Tabulatur verbrochen;
> Meister wird, wen die Prob' nicht reu't."

But here also he must take license, for he must give Walther an opportunity to become Master, and so to win Eva's hand. Hence he brings in some motives from the ceremony of receiving

---

1) Mey, 90 ff.

an apprentice into the Mastersingers Guild.¹) The roll-call occurred only in the Singing-school, and it was only the Singing-school which held its sessions in church. The first question which is asked of Walther, however,
„ist er frei und ehrlich geboren?"
comes from the rules for taking in an apprentice, which was done at the Revel. The other two questions really have no basis in Wagenseil.

This meeting was, however, according to Wagner, not a regular meeting at all, but a gathering preliminary to the public festival of St. John's day. This public festival of the Mastersingers is no invention, as we learn from the Nuremberg „Schulzettel", and of course it was necessary to arrange for the occcasion at some previous meeting. The letter of foundation of the Freiburg School (1513)²) says that there shall be two Singing-schools, one on St. John Evangelist's day and the other on the Tuesday of Whitsuntide. There must have been a meeting of this sort on St. John Evangelist's day in Nuremberg also, to the preparation for which Hans Sachs refers:³)

„Item alle jar auf sanct thomas tag oder die nechst schuel darfor sol man die Festlider verhören und die fest singer verornern (verordnen) wie solen singen."

This was evidently to prepare for a festival on St. John Evangelist's Day (December 27). According to Schnorr von Carolsfeld⁴) there was a festal gathering of the Mastersingers at Wöhrd, a suburb of Nuremberg, on the Feast of Trinity. Now Wagner has either mistaken the festival of St. John Evangelist for that of St. John Baptist (June 24) or has arbitrarily changed the festival of Trinity to that of St. John. His reasons for choosing this spring-day, so beautifully celebrated in southern Germany, are obvious.

---

1) Wagenseil, 546.
2) Uhland: „Schriften", II, 297.¦
3) Genée, 412.
4) Mey, 44, Ranisch, 28, says that the Nuremberg Mastersingers had a festival a week after Pentecostal Sunday at Wöhrd — but this was because the expenses of meeting in the church were too great.

Wagner has also arbitrarily assumed that there were two Critic's Seats (Gemerke), a smaller and a larger, the first to be used at the Open Singing, the second in the Singing-school (VII, 164). This is a gratuitous invention of his, as is also the marking of the song by Beckmesser as the only critic, instead of the customary three or four. This latter device was however necessary, since only Walther's rival would have criticized his song so severely. Poor Walther is marked, too, according to rules that he has never heard, for from the Leges Tabulaturæ have been read to him only the introductory part, and David's glib enumeration of errors contains no real information.

There is a curious slip in Hans Sachs' speech immediately after his reception by the apprentices and people in the third act. Sachs informs the people (VII, 261):

„Schon grosse Ehr' ward mir erkannt,
ward heut' ich zum Spruchsprecher ernannt:
und was mein Spruch euch künden soll,
glaubt, das ist hoher Ehre voll!"

Now as a matter of fact, a „Spruchsprecher" was a droll fellow, standing between the fool of the middle ages and the clown of today, who improvised at weddings and such occassions songs both pertinent and impertinent. How Wagner could have made this a position of honor, conveying the idea that the „Spruchsprecher" was the mouth-piece of the Mastersinger's body, is a mystery, for Wagenseil[1]) gives a long list of reasons why the „Spruchsprecher" were not to be confounded with the Mastersingers, which are briefly as follows:

1. They were single sporadic occurrences in various cities and had no organization, no were they legitimatized by the authorities.

2) They always improvised, and hence their verses were forced and irregular, bound by no rules, as were those of the Mastersingers.

3. They were „gute nasse Brüder", and sang for money or drink at weddings and other festal gatherings, their verses flowing in proportion to the flow of ardent spirits.

---
1) Wagenseil, 488 ff.

4. They altered words to suit themselves for the sake of the rime, and did not confine themselves to the strict truth, as for instance Wilhelm Weber, the great Nuremberg „Spruchsprecher", said:

„Paulus schreibt an die Epheser,
Ihr Herren seid lustig, brecht aber keine Gläser."

5. They were boorish, and in their songs attacked things high and low, secular and religious, so that in some cities they were suppressed by the magistracy.

6. They either spoke their doggerel, or sang it in only one ballad-melody.

7. Their only object was to excite laughter.

8. They were esteemed only by the rabble, while Mastersingers were held in honor by people of rank.

9. There were no learned men among them, as among the Mastersingers.

There remains the possibility of crediting Wagner with an intentional and therefore humorous misuse of the term. Hans Sachs may be saying all this quite jokingly. If this interpretation be true, it must be said that very few of the audience will be likely ever to know that this is a joke.

There remains one point to notice which is a little out of the province of our theme, but which is mentioned for the sake of completeness. Wagner has not only borrowed literally for his text from Wagenseil, but for his score as well. Two of his motives in the Overture are taken from the melodies of the crowned Mastertunes given in Wagenseil.

The first motive occurs in the fourteenth measure of the Overture.[1])

Wagenseil: „Das dritte Gesetz, im langen Thon Ludwig Marner":

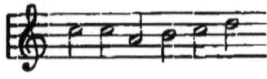

---

1) Wagner: „Die Meistersinger von Nürnberg", „Clavierauszug von Karl Tausig", 1.

Wagner:

The same motive is repeated in the two following measures.

Again, at the beginning of the pompous Mastersingers' March, is given a variant of the whole tone-progression from the beginning of the Long Tune of Heinrich Mügling.

Wagenseil:

This movement is introduced in Wagner by the trumpets and harps, is repeated twice and a half, then in the eighth following measure is given once and a half again.

Wagner:[1])

---

1) „Clavierausgabe", p. 3. cf. also Heinz: „The Mastersingers of Nuremberg", 5 ff.

CHAPTER II.
SOURCES OF THE PLOT OF THE „MASTER-SINGERS".

How many sources are drawn upon for one masterwork is hard to say. The germ of a composition swells oftentimes when the artist himself is not aware of it, and who can watch the process of this unconscious growing? We enquire first about the seed when we see the flower. The „Mastersingers" has its roots back in Wagner's boyhood.

I. TRACES OF E. T. A. HOFFMANN IN THE „MASTERSINGERS".

Muncker, in his excellent although brief life of Wagner, speaks more than once of the influence on Wagner of the romantic novelist E. T. A. Hoffmann. From his early youth [1], Wagner was familiar with the tales of this eccentric genius (at once artist, writer, and musician), and it was to this German Poe that he owed suggestions for at least two of his operas, i. e. „Tannhäuser" and the „Mastersingers". The two novels written by Wagner during his first dreary stay in Paris „Eine Pilgerfahrt zu Beethoven" and „Ein Ende in Paris" bear likewise many traces of Hoffmann.

„Einzelne Züge in diesem vortrefflich erzählten, mit Witz, Humor, Ironie und Satire gewürzten, aber auch mit rührender Empfindung reich erfüllten Novellen, muten uns in ihrer wunderlichen Genialität geradezu Hoffmannisch an." [2]

---
1) Muncker: „Richard Wagner", 7.
2) Ibid. 23.

In 1842 Wagner began „Tannhäuser", whose plot contains some motives from Hoffmann's „Kampf der Sänger".[1]) In 1845 he finished this work and went during the summer to Marienbad to recuperate. It was here that he made the first sketch of the „Mastersingers", still under the influence of his studies for „Tannhäuser", and it is perhaps from the „Kampf der Sänger" that he first came upon a mention of Wagenseil, his indispensible source for all that pertains to Mastersong.

The story of Hoffmann's to which Wagner owes the main motive of the plot of the „Mastersinger" is „Meister Martin der Küfner und seine Gesellen",[2]) originally published in the „Leipzig Taschenbuch zum geselligen Vergnügen" in 1819, and afterwords inserted in his collected works as one of the short novels in the „Serapionsbrüder". The scene of this story is ancient Nuremberg, at the time when Mastersong was in its prime. The plot is briefly as follows:

Master Martin, the richest and most honorable cooper of Nuremberg, and Candlemaster of his guild, has a beautiful daughter Rosa, whom he purposes to marry only to that journeyman who shall excell in his own calling of coopering. This resolution is, as he believes, in accordance with a divine revelation made to him by his grandmother on her death-bed, on the night of Rosa's birth — a communication which ran as follows:

„Mägdlein zart mit rothen Wangen,
Rosa, hör das Gebot,
Magst dich wahren vor Noth und Bangen.
— — — — — — — T —
Ein glänzend Häuslein wird er bringen,
Würzige Fluthen treiben drinn,
Blanke Englein gar lustig singen,
Mit frommen Sinn
Horch treuster Minn.
Ha! lieblichen Liebesklingen.

---

1) Muncker: „Richard Wagner", 36.
2) Hoffmann: „Gesammelte Schriften", II, 224.

Das Häuslein mit güldnen Prangen,
Der hat's ins Haus getrag'n,
Den wirst du süss umfangen,
Darf'fst nicht den Vater frag'n
Ist dein Bräut'gam minniglich.
Ins Haus das Häuslein bringt allwegen
Reichthum, Glück, Heil und Hort" u. s. w.[1])

Master Martin sees clearly that this vessel, in which are spicy juices, and angels singing up and down, can be no other than a wine-cask, and that the angels are the pearling drops, hence his decision.

Now three youths, Friedrich, a silversmith, Reinhold, an artist, and Conrad, the son of a country noble, all fall in love with Rosa, and knowing Master Martin's condition for winning her, all three learn the cooper's trade and enter his service as journeymen-apprentices.[2]) Friedrich finally wins the maiden, not by making a fine cask, but by fashioning in his leisure hours a curiously beautiful silver goblet, which contains the spicy wine as well as a cask, and in the bottom of which are chased the figures of angels, which seem to float up and down as the wine bubbles over them.

Hoffmann introduces also an Open-Singing in the church of St. Catharine, in which Friedrich and Reinhold take part, to the great delight of the Mastersingers. When he wrote his own drama, Wagner may have had in mind the following sentence:

„Bald darauf setzte sich Friedrich auf den Singstuhl, zog sein Barett ab und begann, nachdem er einige Sekunden vor sich hingeschaut, dann aber einen Blick in die Versammlung geworfen, der wie ein glühender Pfeil der holden Rosa in die Brust traf, dass sie tief aufseufzen musste, ein solches herrliches Lied im zarten Ton Heinrich Frauenlob's, dass alle Meister einmüthiglich

---

1) Hoffmann, II, 242.

2) This story was suggested to Hoffmann by a picture of Kolbe's, representing the interior of a cooper's shop with a master-cooper and his three young apprentices working, and a maiden just entering the door. This picture Hoffmann represents as being given to Rosa as a wedding-present by Reinhold. See Ellinger: „E. T. A. Hoffmann", 136.

bekannten, keiner unter ihnen vermöge den jungen Gesellen zu übertreffen."¹)

After the Singing-school Master Martin, his daughter Rosa, and Reinhold and Friedrich go out of the city to the Allerwiese, where games are being played and general festivities are going on. This may have been suggestive to Wagner also of his St. John's day celebration.

But the main point is, that Rosa is offered as a prize for a Masterwork only on condition that she herself consent. Master Martin says:

„Wie es sich künftig fügen mag, überlass ich ganz dem Willen des Herrn, aber so viel ist gewiss, dass weder ein Patrizier, noch ein anderer, meiner Tochter Hand berühren wird, als der Küper, der sich mir als den tüchtigsten geschicktesten Meister bewährt hat. Vorausgesagt, dass ihn meine Tochter mag, denn zwingen werde ich mein liebes Kind zu nichts in der Welt, am wenigsten zu einer Heirath, die ihr nicht ansteht."²)

Now this is precisely the chief motive in Wagner's plot. Eva is to be given to the best master of song, but only if she herself be willing. Pogner says (VII, 173):

„Nun hört noch, wie ich's ernstlich mein'!
Ein' leblos' Gabe stel' ich nicht:
ein Mägdlein sitzt mit zu Gericht.
Den Preis erkennt die Meister-Zunft;
doch gilt's der Eh', so will's Vernunft,
    dass ob der Meister Rath
    die Braut den Ausschlag hat."

There can be no doubt that Wagner drew his principal motive thus from this very tale.

II. THE „MASTERSINGERS" IN ITS RELATION TO DEINHARDSTEIN'S DRAMA „HANS SACHS", AND TO LORTZING'S COMIC OPERA OF THE SAME NAME.

Deinhardstein's drama „Hans Sachs" was given for the first time on the 13th of February, 1828, in the court-theater at

---
1) Hoffmann, II, 269.
2) Ibid. II, 235.

Berlin.¹) A decade later, Lortzing wrote his comic opera of the same name, basing it on Deinhardstein's text. This opera was first given in Leipzig, on the 23rd of June, 1840, on the occasion of the celebration of the four-hundredth anniversary of the invention of printing.²) To each of these plays Wagner perhaps owed something, but to the latter certainly more than to the former.

The plot of Deinhardstein's drama is briefly as follows:

Hans Sachs, a young shoemaker and poet, already a member of the Mastersingers Guild, is in love with Kunigunde,³) the only daughter of Master Steffen, a rich goldsmith in Nuremberg. The maiden returns his affection, but conceals the connection from her father, whose pride would not allow him to give his daughter to a mere cobbler. At this juncture Coban Runge, a councillor from Augsburg, but an egregious coxcomb and coward, sues for the hand of Kunigunde, and is favored by her father on account of his rank. The would-be bridegroom surprises the lovers in a clandestine meeting, and later, finding that his rival is only a shoemaker, reports the matter to Master Steffen just before Hans Sachs comes to demand openly the hand of Kunigunde. Incensed at such presumption, the father is about to refuse Sachs a hearing when the daughter, herself none too well pleased with her lover's lowly calling, declares that Sachs is not a cobbler, and promises to wed Coban that very day if her assertion is not true. At once, in a private interview with Sachs, she demands that he give up his trade in order to gain her hand. This he feels he cannot honorably do, and Kunigunde, mad with disappointment, denies her love for him and bids him begone. Sadly he resolves to leave Nuremberg forever, for also his envious fellows in the Mastersingers guild have put him and his poetry to open shame. Already he is some distance from the city when he meets a stranger in hunting-costume, who enquires the way to Nuremberg. To accommodate this unknown (who is the Emperor

---
1) Deinhardstein: „Hans Sachs", 5.
2) Lortzing: „Hans Sachs", 5 f.
3) Kunigunde Creutzerin, the only daughter of Peter Creutzer, was Hans Sachs' first wife. See Ranisch, 39.

Maximilian travelling incognito), be turns back, learning on the way to his great satisfaction that his poetry has reached the ears of the Emperor and found favor there. In the meantime Master Steffen has been elected burgomaster, which honor Runge cleverly persuades him is due to his efforts. The grateful burgomaster decides to give him Kunigunde that very day as his reward. The young lady, however, opposes this arrangement; force is about to be employed when Sachs re-appears on the scene. He hastens to Maximilian, whom be believes to be a powerful duke, and receives from him a half-promise of assistance if he will repair an hour hence to the market-place, where a festival is being held in honor of the installation of the new burgomaster. Here he learns in a stolen interview with the repentant Kunigunde that the burgomaster and the city fathers have passed sentence of banishment on him on account of his forcible entrance into Master Steffen's garden. Just then Maximilian appears, and under color of a suppositious case which he proposes to the burgomaster he makes that worthy decide his own case in favor of Sachs and Kunigunde. Master Steffen still urges, however, the claims of gratitude which Coban has upon him, but the councillors assure him that Coban had nothing to do with their choice. Coban slinks off: Sachs is crowned with a laurel-wreath by Kunigunde and the play ends in uproarious cheers for Emperor Max.

Wagner certainly must have known this drama, but is apparently not directly indebted to it.[1]) Most of the motives which are common to Deinhardstein and Wagner occur in Lortzing also. We note a few exceptions. Walther's Prizesong 'recalls one of Sachs' monologues in Deinhardstein:[2])

„Wie leer erscheint mir jetzt der Traum,
Als einmal unterm Blütenbaum,
Sich mir der Dichtkunst Muse zeigte,
Den Lorbeer mir herunterneigte;
Dies schöne Bild der Phantasie,
Es wich aus meiner Seele nie."

---

1) „Richard Wagner-Jahrbuch", I, 236 f.
2) Deinhardstein, 66.

This idea, as it is in Deinhardstein, probably comes from Hans Sachs himself[1]) and it is hardly crediting Wagner with too much poetical ingenuity to suppose that he may have hit on this common motive independently. This does not seem to me necessarily to prove knowledge on his part of Deinhardstein's drama.

The character of Hans Sachs, as he appears in the „Mastersingers", is also foreshadowed to some degree in Deinhardstein. He is represented already in this drama as in revolt in some degree against the barren rules of Mastersong in favor of more truly poetic expression. A criticism[2]) of him put in the mouth one of the Mastersingers would serve as an excellent comment on Hans Sachs and his attitude toward Walther's poetry as depicted in the „Mastersingers".

„Zweiter Meistersinger. Er hat Talent,
Das ist wohl wahr — allein —
Erster Meistersinger. Talent! Talent!
Wir brauchen kein Talent, Tabulaturam
Soll er befolgen; die Aequivoca,
Die Relativa und die blinden Worte
Soll er vermeiden, keine Milben brauchen,
Glatt singen soll er, das begehren wir,
Nicht aber dabei zucken, wie er's thut,
Das macht den Dichter und nicht das Talent.
Talent kann jeder haben, aber nicht
Das rechte Ohr und jene Sorgsamkeit,
So uns die Fehler klug vermeiden lassen,
Und die sprech ich ihm ab: er ist noch nicht
Gesetzt genug, ihm macht die Phantasie
Zu vielen Schaden noch."

The closing scene of both plays is also in so far similar, as that the heroine crowns the hero with a wreath. This incident is not repeated in Lortzing, but as we have shown above, Wagner has evidently taken this from Wagenseil.

---

1) Sachs: „Gesammelte Werke". VII, 202 ff., in the „Gesprech, die neun gab Muse oder Kunstgöttin betreffend".
2) Deinhardstein, 15.

We turn now to Lortzing, whose opera affords a more satisfactory field for comparison.

The text to Lortzing's opera was written for the most part by his friend the actor Philipp Reger. A few of the humorous touches Lortzing himself added. The song with the refrain: „Der Liebe Glück, das Vaterland" (No. 1) and the finale, were written by Philipp Düringer.[1])

The plot of the opera is as follows:

Hans Sachs, a young shoemaker and Mastersinger of Nuremberg, already well-known throughout Germany as a poet, has sued successfully for the love of Kunigunde, the daughter of the rich goldsmith Master Steffen. Sachs' happiness is clouded, however, by the arrival of Coban Hesse, councillor in Augsburg, who obtains from Master Steffen the promise of his daughter's hand. The already arrogant goldsmith becomes still more puffed up by his election as burgomaster, and in an open contest in the Singing-school between Sachs and Coban Hesse he gives the prize to the latter, as well as the public assurance of his daughter's hand. To this the jealous Mastersingers readily assent, although the people are unanimous for Sachs. During the same festival Görg, Sachs' apprentice, who is in love with Kordula, Kunigunde's cousin, in honor of his lady-love on her birthday, reads as his own a poem which he has stolen from Sachs. This manuscript he afterward loses, but it is picked up by two of the Emperor's archers, and carried to Maxmilian himself, who is already an admirer of Sachs' poetry, and who has recently visited him in his shop incognito. In the meantime Sachs, justly incensed at his public humiliation, resolves to leave Nuremberg. His farewell interview with Kunigunde is unfortunately discovered by the burgomaster, who by virtue of his office passes upon him at once sentence of banishment. Sachs leaves, accompanied by his faithful Görg, but, meeting on the way Emperor Maxmilian, whom he recognizes only as his unknown visitor, returns in his train to Nuremberg. On his arrival, the Emperor causes enquiries to be made concerning the

---

1) Lortzing, 6 f.

author of the manuscript which has come into his hands. In collusion with his future father-in-law, Coban boldly declares himself the author. The Emperor requests him to prove his claim by delivering the poem. This of course Coban cannot do, so the Emperor orders Hans Sachs to appear, and proclaims him the author. Amid the jubilations of the people he is again received among them, and is promised the hand of Kunigunde. The Emperor admonishes the citizens not to scorn the shoemaker poet on account of his humble calling, and amid huzzas for Maxmilian the curtain drops.

In this plot we recognize at once many motives of the „Mastersingers". The indebtedness may be summarized as follows:

In each play occurs a representation of a singing-contest in one of the Mastersingers meetings, and in each the hero composes a Mastersong on the stage. In „Hans Sachs" Görg purloins his master's poem, in order to win Kordula's approbation. In the „Mastersingers" Beckmesser steals Walther's poem (believing it to be Hans Sachs's), in order to win the hand of Eva. In „Hans Sachs" Coban Hesse, the pretended author of the poem, fails to deliver it, and is thereby put to shame. In the „Mastersingers" Beckmesser fails in the same test, and suffers the same defeat. In both plays the hero is revealed as the real author, and thereby gains the hand of the heroine. Kunigunde and Kordula[1]) in the one opera, correspond to Eva and Magdalene in the other. In „Hans Sachs" Görg, Sachs' apprentice, is in love with Kordula, Kunigunda's cousin, just as in the „Mastersingers" David is in love with Magdalene. In both operas the apprentice makes great pretensions to a knowledge of Mastersong, and is derided by his comrades for his sloth and vanity. In both operas occur apprentice-choruses[2]) and cobbler-songs.[3]) Coban Hesse sings a stupid Mastersong of his own composition, with which may be compared Beckmesser's serenade.[4]) The mono-

---

1) This pair is undoubtedly taken from Agathe and Aennchen in von Weber's „Freischütz".
2) Lortzing, 1 f. Wagner, VII, 165 f. and 191 f.
3) Lortzing, 11 and 43. Wagner, VII, 211 ff., 232 and 258.
4) Lortzing, 35 f. Wagner, VII, 219 ff.

logue[1]) of Hans Sachs in Lortzing finds a refined echo in Sachs's monologue in the „Mastersingers".

Lortzing:
„Wo bist Du, Sachs? Hat Dich ein Traum umfangen?
Ist, armer Sterblicher, Dir schon die Pforte
Zum sel'gen Jenseits aufgegangen?
Das kann nicht Leben sein — das ist kein Traum,
Und dennoch wachend fass' ich's kaum!
Was ich in mitternächt'gen Stunden
Gedacht, gefühlt, empfunden,
In and'ren Herzen fand es Widerklang —

— — — — — — — —

Doch nun zur Ruh', bewegt' Gemüth,
Du musst dies Treiben unterlassen,
Und was Dich hin zur Erde zieht,
Musst Du mit ernstem Sinn erfassen.
  (Tritt an den Arbeitstisch.)
Dem Meister Brass versprach ich neue Schuhe
In nächster Frist, drum rasch an's Werk."

Wagner:
„Wie duftet doch der Flieder
so mild, so stark und voll!
Mir lös't er weich die Glieder,
will, dass ich 'was sagen soll. —
Was gibt's, was ich dir sagen kann?
Bin gar ein arm einfältig Mann!
Soll mir die Arbeit nicht schmecken,
gäbst, Freund, lieber mich frei:
thät besser das Leder zu strecken,
und liess' all Poeterei! —
  (Er versucht wieder zu arbeiten. Lässt ab und sinnt.)
Und doch, 's will halt nicht geh'n. —
Ich fühl's — und kann's nicht versteh'n; —
kann's nicht behalten, — doch auch nicht vergessen;
und fass ich es ganz, — kann ich's nicht messen. —

---

[1] Lortzing, 15 f. (Nr. 2. Scene and Aria.) Wagner, VII, 197 f.

> Doch wie auch wollt' ich's fassen,
> was unermesslich mir schien?
> Kein' Regel wollte da passen,
> und war doch kein Fehler drin." —

With all this undeniable carrying-over of motives, Wagner is no plagiarist. It is the right of the present generation to rest on the shoulders of the preceding one, and if by so doing it gains a clearer outlook, so much the better. Wagner's text infinitely surpasses Lortzing's, both in literary form, and in historical accuracy and vividness. Thus in the details of the play he gives us a far more careful and characteristic picture of the time of which he writes than his predecessors in the same field. In plot, he is superior to an equal degree. In removing Sachs from the position of hero, he has given us a beautiful historical ideal of the Nuremberg singer, unmared by the pettiness of a young lover's passion, a genial and benignant character, yet withal with that tinge of melancholy, coming from his hardly self-confessed love for Eva, which is the final touch of art in all portrayal.

As he sits in his workshop on the morning of St. John's Day, reading the great folio on his knees, we can think of him only as his pupil Adam Puschman depicts him, in his benignant old age:[1)]

> „Ein Alt Man, was
> Grau und weis, wie ein Taub dermas,
> Der het ein grossen Bart fürbas
> In ein schönen grossen Buch las
> Mit Gold beschlagen schön.

This is the great point in which Wagner excells the others. But he has also ennobled the character of the heroine's father by representing him not as influenced by pride in the disposal of his daughter's hand, but by a worthy desire to advance the interests of his beloved Mastersong.

---

1) From Puschman's „Elogium Reverendi Viri Johannis Sachsen Noribergensis", printed as supplement to Ranisch, 358.

III. HAGEN'S „NORICA".

Muncker¹) mentions also as a source from which Wagner may have drawn for our drama Hagen's historical novel „Norica", which first appeared in 1829. This novel purports to be an account by one Heller, merchant of Frankfurt, of his visit to Nuremberg in 1518. The time is slightly earlier than that of the „Mastersingers", and the novel is really a series of pictures of the famous artists of Nuremberg. — Dürer, the painter, Veit Stoss, the wood-carver, Peter Vischer, the brass-founder, Adam Krafft, the sculptor, and others whose labors served to make Nuremberg the most beautiful of mediaeval German cities. Hans Sachs is introduced as a rollicking young cobbler (he would have been thirty-four at this time), and a description of the Singing-school and of the Revel of the Mastersingers finds its due place. It is not difficult to see that Wagenseil was Hagen's source here, as well as Wagner's, the surest evidence being that he repeats the mistakes of his authority, i. e. gives Ketner's name as Kothner ²) and puts the Singing-school in St. Catharine's church at this early day.³)

I can find no evidence that Wagner used this novel. If he had followed it very closely, he would have avoided his own anachronism in regard to Hans Folz, whose time Hagen gives distinctly as fifty years before that of Hans Sachs.⁴)

IV. DIRECT QUOTATIONS.

Wagner has twice availed himself of the privilege of direct quotation in his text, outside of the already-mentioned pariphrase of a portion of Wagenseil. The first that we have to note is the song with which the people greet Sachs on his arrival at the festival in the Pegnitz-meadow (VII, 260). This song, „Die

---

1) Muncker: „Richard Wagner", 84.
2) Hagen: „Norica", 246.
3) Ibid. 243.
4) Ibid. 237.

Wittembergische Nachtigal", [1]) is characteristic of Sachs' attitude toward the Reformation. Almost from the very first he took an interest in it, buying numerous Reformation pamphlets which he had bound together in 1522. At the end of the volume he had written: "Dieses Püchlein habe ich Hans Sachs also gesamelt, Gott und seinem Wort zu Ehren und dem Nächsten zu gut einpünden lassen, als man zählt nach Christi Gepurt 1522 Jahr. Die Wahrheit bleibt ewiglich." [2]) The "Wittembergisch Nachtigall" followed in 1523. The epithet which he gave Luther was taken up by both friends and enemies, and he himself was subjected to abuse. Thus Cochläus writes in his "Actis Lutheri" "Auch Schuster und Weiber lasen das N. Testament D. Luthers begierig und konnten es fast auswendig." [3]) Not content with this, Sachs published the following year four prose dialogues, treating the theme of the hour in a popular theological style. For several years after this Sachs was silent, but finally he was induced by Osiander, the fiery Reformation preacher in the church of St. Lawrence, to add verses to a number of pictures, found in a Carthusian cloister in Nuremberg after its revocation. The pictures were printed as woodcuts, bearing the names of Hans Sachs and Osiander, under the title "Ein wunderlicher Weissagung vom Papstthum", in 1527.[4]) The book was offered for sale in the Nuremberg market, but at once the copies were confiscated so far as possible by the city council, and Osiander and Sachs, as well as the printer, received a severe reprimand and a warning against any such further attempt. This effectually silenced Sachs' Reformation songs for almost a decade, and when he did begin again, it was in a milder ard more general tone.

The theme of this song was treated by Hans Sachs both as a "Spruchgedicht" and as a Mastersong, and was a popular Reformation-song throughout Germany. The lines are given literally by Wagner. The false rime in the last two lines is

---

1) Sachs: "Gesammelte Werke", VI, 368 ff.
2) Genée, 136.
3) Ibid. 143.
4) Ibid. 165 ff.

caused by the transference into modern orthography of the original, which reads as follows: [1])

„Die rotprünstige morgenröt
Her durch die trüben wolcken göt" —

The second quotation is the night-watchman's song. Erk and Böhme [2]) give it as a call in Thuringia and Saxony, which goes back to the sixteenth century at least, and was still to be heard up to 1858. Wagner incorporates in his opera both text and melody substantially as they were to be heard in his boyhood in Saxony. The second verse (VII, 229) is a humorous addition of Wagner's own.

---

[1] Sachs: „Gesammelte Werke", VI, 368 ff.
[2] „Deutscher Liederhort", III, 411.

CHAPTER III.
HISTORY AND COMPARISON OF THE VARIOUS TEXTS.

I. THE FACSIMILE TEXT.

The first suggestion for the „Mastersingers" came to Wagner in connection with his studies for „Tannhäuser", which was first performed in 1845.[1]) In his „Mittheilung an meine Freunde"[2]) he gives a sketch of its origin and first form. In this sketch several important elements of the plot are not mentioned. In the first place, Eva's freedom to reject an unwelcome suitor is not referred to. Then the listener to Beckmesser's serenade is not named, and there is no allusion to the cudgeling scene which ends the second act. Neither David nor Magdalene are introduced. On the other hand, there is one considerable variation in plot, i. e. Beckmesser demands a new song from Sachs, the morning after the serenade, on the ground that Sachs has spoiled the effect of his own song on Eva; and Sachs thereupon gives him Walther's song, professing however not to know whence it came. The rest of the plot goes on as in the published version.

Wagner's attention was soon drawn off from this projected work. In 1849, on account of political difficulties, he was obliged to flee to Zürich, where he remained for ten years.[3]) In 1855 „Lohengrin" was given for the first time, and in 1859 „Tristan and Isolde" was completed. In the same year he visited Paris, where the famous, or rather infamous „Tannhäuser" fiasco

---
1) Glasenapp: „Richard Wagner's Leben und Wirken", I, 208 ff.
2) Wagner, IV, 385 ff. This account was published in 1851.
3) Glasenapp, I, 265 ff.

occurred.¹) In 1861 Wagner settled in Vienna, and on the 30th of October of this year he wrote to his publishers (Schott) in Mayence, offering them the text and score of the „Mastersingers" ready for performance in the following winter.²)

On the 19th of November 1861 he sent the prose-sketch of the plot to his publishers. Two manuscripts of this sketch are in existence, one in the possession of B. Schott's Sons, in Mayence, the other belonging to Frau Cosima Wagner, and in Villa Wahnfried, Bayreuth. As the plot is the same as in the later poetical versions, an outline of it is not necessary.³) It was not until the 25th of September, 1862, that Wagner (then at Biebrich on the Rhine) sent the manuscript of the text to Mayence. Toward Christmas, 1862, this text was published in manuscript. This has been recently reprinted,³) and affords a chance for comparison with the later text. The variations from the printed text in his collected works are numerous and striking, showing the gradual improvement of the plot. The variations of the two texts have been printed in part,⁵) but never completely. The following list gives all differences except those in the stage-directions.

Facsimile-Edition.	Second Printed Edition.
2. [In this edition do not appear the names of the last six Master-singers.]	
7. „Für euch Leben und Blut! Für euch dichtender Muth!"	157. „Für euch Gut und Blut! Für euch Dichter 's heil'ger Muth!"
7. „liebende Huth."	158. „liebesheil'ge Huth."

---

1) Glasenapp, II, 56 ff.
2) „Nord und Süd", LXXII, 220 ff.
3) I am indebted to the courtesy of the publishers named for information on this point.
4) In 1895. The date is not given in the book.
5) In „Nord und Süd" LXXII, 220 ff., and in „Bayreuther Blätter", XV, 225 ff.

Facsimile-Edition.	Second Printed Edition.
10. „der ‚Lerchen'-, der ‚Schnecken'-, der ‚Beller'-Ton, der ‚verwirrte' Ton, der ‚Töne'-Ton."	189. „der ‚Lerchen'-, der Schnecken'-, der ‚Beller'-Ton."
10. „als gut es die Stimm' erreichen kann"	162. „als es die Stimm' erreichen kann."
17. „Pogner Veit".	„Pogner Veit! Alle Zeit, weit und breit: Pogner Veit!"
18. „ob in der Gewohnheit trock'nem Geleise."	174. „ob in der Gewohnheit trägem G'leise.
18. „ihr selbst euch wendet zu dem Volk. Ein Frei-Singen wird gehalten; und obgleich immer die Regeln walten, nach Lust und Laune, ungequält, Stoff und Vers Jeder sich erwählt: dem Volke soll's behagen."	175. „ihr selbst euch wendet zu dem Volk', Dem Volke wollt ihr behagen."
21. „Meint, Junker, ihr in Sang und Dicht'."	179. Meint, Junker, hier in Sang' und Dicht'."
22. „Ein Gesetz besteht aus zweier Stollen"	181. „Ein Gesetz besteht aus zweenen Stollen[1])
23. „von tausend holden Stimmen	182. „von holder Stimmen Gemenge.
Zum Glockenhall wird das Gesumm' der Immen!"	Wie Glockenhall ertöst des Jubel's Gedränge!"
24. „der neues Leben mir schuf: nun stimm' ich an"	183. „der neu ihr Leben schuf: stimmt nun an."

---

1) A more correct form for the dative plural. „Zweier" is properly genitive.

Facsimile-Edition.	Second Printed Edition.
25. „hörtet ihr besser zu, Dem Junker, der vor euch verlor, ihm gabt ihr sieben Fehler vor: doch eines Meistergesanges Bar gab euch der Jüngling vor; dass der ganz glatt nach den Regeln war, das entging des Merker's Ohr. **Vogelgesang.** Zwei Stollen fand ich wohlgericht'. **Nachtigal.** Auch der Abgesang entging mir nicht. **Sachs.** Als er der Fragen Antwort gab, stellt' er ein Bar nach Maass und Stab. **Kothner.** Nur die Weise war ganz confus. **Sachs.** Darum,[1]) so komm' ich jetzt zum Schluss."	186. „hörtet ihr besser zu
26. „Beckmesser. Nichts weiter! Zum Schluss! **Die Meister.** Genug! zum Schluss!"	186. „Darum, so komm' ich jetzt zum Schluss." 181. „Die Meister. Genug! zum Schluss!"
28. „auf da steigt"	189. „auf das steigt."

---

1) By the ommission of these lines the significance of the „darum" in Sach's speech is somewhat obscured.

Facsimile-Edition.	Second Printed Edition.
32. „H'm! h'm! — Was geht mir im Kopf doch 'rum?"	195. „H'm! — Was geht mir im Kopf doch 'rum?"
36. „Ohne Gnad' versang der Rittersmann".	202. „Ohne Gnad' versang der Herr Rittersmann."
40. „damit dem Nachbar kein Schad' geschicht!"	208. „Damit Niemand kein Schad' geschicht."
41. „Ach, neue Noth!"	210. „Ach! meine Noth." [1])
48. „Sich einen guten frischen Muth."	220. „sich einen guten und frischen Muth."
51. „zu Hülfe! Zu Hülfe!"	224. „Zu Hilfe! zu Hilfe!"

THE STREET-FIGHT.

52. „Kennt man die Schlosser nicht? Sie haben's angericht'!" — Nein, dort die Schmiede mit Kloben und Niete! — Die Becker! die Becker! Die Ofenhöcker! — Meinst du etwa mich? Mein ich wohl dich? — Seht nur, der Hase! hat überall die Nase!" — Da hast's auf die Schnautze! — Herr, jetzt setzt's Plautze!"	229. „Kennt man die Schlosser nicht? Die haben's sicher angericht'! — Ich glaub' die Schmiede werden's sein. — Die Schreiner seh' ich dort beim Schein. — Hei! Schau die Schäffler dort beim Tanz. — Dort seh' die Bader ich im Glanz. Krämer finden sich zur Hand. mit Gerstenstang und Zuckerkand; mit Pfeffer, Zimmt, Muscatennuss. Sie riechen schön, sie riechen schön, doch haben viel Verdruss, und bleiben gern vom Schuss. —

---

1) One is tempted to believe that „meine" is here a misprint for „neue". The latter is at any rate more significant.

Facsimile-Edition.	Second Printed Edition.
	Seht nur, der Hase
	hat üb'rall die Nase! —
	Meinst du damit etwa mich?
	Mein ich damit etwa dich?
	Da hat's auf die Schnauze! —
	Heu, jetzt setzt's Plautze! —
	Hei! Krach! Hagelwetter-
	schlag!
	Wo das sitzt, da wachst
	nichts nach! —
	Keilt euch wacker,
	haut die Racker!
	Haltet selbst Gesellen Stand;
	wer da wich, 's war wahrlich
	Schand'!
	Drauf und dran!
	Wie ein Mann
	steh'n wir alle zur Keilerei!
Gesellen und Bürger	Gesellen.
	Heda! Gesellen 'ran!
	Dort wird mit Streit und Zank
	gethan
	Da giebt's gewiss gleich Schlä-
	gerei;
	Gesellen, haltet euch dabei!
'Sind die Weber und Gerber!	's sind die Weber und Gerber!
Dacht' ich's doch gleich! —	Dacht' ich's doch gleich! —
Die Preisverderber!	Die Preisverderber!
Spielen immer Streich'!	Spielen immer Streich'!
Dort den Metzger Klaus,	Dort den Metzger Klaus,
den kennt man heraus! —	den kennt man heraus! —
'S ist morgen der Fünfte!	
brennt manchem im Haus.	
Zünfte! Zünfte!	Zünfte! Zünfte!
Zünfte heraus!	Zünfte heraus! —

Facsimile-Edition.	Second Printed Edition.
Schneider mit dem Bügel!	Schneider mit dem Bügel!
Hei, hier setzt's Prügel!	Hei, hie setzt's Prügel!
Gürtler! — Zinngiesser! —	Gürtler! — Zinngiesser! —
Leimsieder! — Lichtgiesser! —	Leimsieder! — Lichtgiesser! —
Tuchscherer her!	Tuchscherer her!
Leinweber her!	Leinweber her!
Hierher! hierher!	Hieher! Hieher!
Immer mehr! Immer mehr!	Immer mehr! Immer mehr!
	Nun tüchtig drauf! Wir schlagen los!
	jetzt wird die Keilerei erst gross! —
	Lauft heim, sonst kriegt ihr's von der Frau;
	hier giebt's nur Prügel-Färbeblau!
	Immer 'ran!
	Mann für Mann!
	Schlagt sie nieder!
	Zünfte! Zünfte! Heraus! —
	Die Meister.
	Was giebt's denn für Zank und Streit?
	Das tos't ja weit und breit!
	Gebt Ruh' und scheer' sich Jeder heim,
	sonst schlag' ein Hageldonnerwetter drein!
	Stemmt euch hier nicht mehr zu Hauf',
	oder sonst wir schlagen drauf.
Die Nachbarinnen.	
	Was ist denn da für Streit und Zank?
	's wird einem wahrlich angst und bang!

Facsimile-Edition.	Second Printed Edition.
	Da ist mein Mann gewiss dabei,
	gewiss kommt's noch zur Schlägerei!
He da! dort unten!	He da! Ihr dort unten
Seid doch gescheit!	so seid doch nur gescheit!
Seid ihr gleich Alle	Seid ihr zu Streit und Raufen
zum Streite bereit?	gleich Alle so bereit?
Was für ein Zanken und Toben!	Was für ein Zanken und Toben!
Da werden schon Arme erhoben.	Da werden schon Arme erhoben!
Hört doch! Hört doch!	Hört doch! Hört doch!
Seid ihr denn toll?	Seid ihr denn toll?
Sind euch die Köpfe	Sind euch die Köpfe
von Weine noch voll?	vom Weine noch voll?
Zu Hülfe! Zu Hülfe!	Zu Hilfe! Zu Hilfe!
Da schlägt sich mein Mann	Da schlägt sich mein Mann!
Der Vater! Der Vater!	Der Vater! Der Vater!
Sieht man das an!	Sieht man das an?
Christian! Peter!	Christian! Peter!
Niklaus! Hans!	Niklaus! Hans!
Auf! schreit Zeter!	Auf! Schreit Zeter!
Hörst du nicht, Franz?	Hörst du nicht, Franz?
Gott! wie sie walken!	Gott, wie sie walken!
's wackeln die Zöpfe!	's wackeln die Zöpfe!
Wasser her! Wasser her!	Wasser her! Wasser her!
Giesst's ihn' auf die Köpfe!	Giesst's ihn' auf die Köpfe!
	Magdalena.
	Ach Himmel! Meine Noth ist gross!
	David! So hör mich doch nur an!
	So lass' doch nur den Herren los!
	Er hat mir ja nichts gethan."

Facsimile-Edition.	Second Printed Edition.
53a. „Hätt' ich nur Wurst und Kuchen fort!"	231. „Hätt' ich nur die Wurst und den Kuchen fort!" —
	232. „(Er hat in der Zerstreung die Worte der Melodie von Beckmesser's Werbelied aus dem vorausgehenden Aufzuge gesungen; Sachs macht eine verwunderte Bewegung, worauf David sich unterbricht.) Verzeiht, Meister; ich kam in's Gewirr'; Der Polterabend machte mich irr'. (Er fährt nun in der richtigen Melodie fort): Am Jordan Sankt Johannes stand"
54. „an der Pegnitz is der Hans"	232. „an der Pegnitz hiess der Hans."
54. „Wahn und Wahn!"	233. „Wahn! Wahn!"
56. „Gott weiss, wie das geschah? Ein Kobold half wohl da? Der Flieder war's: Johannisnacht, drob ist der Wahn so leicht erwacht. Ein Glühwurm fand sein Weibchen nicht; der hat den Schaden angericht': ängstlich suchend flog er dahin durch manches müde Menschenhirn; dem knistert's nun wie Funk und Feuer, die Welt steht dem in Brand	„und will's der Wahn geseg'nen, nun muss es Prügel regnen, mit Hieben, Stöss und Dreschen, den Wuthesbrand zu löschen. Gott weiss, wie das geschah? — Ein Kobold half wohl da! Ein Glühwurm fand sein Weibchen nicht; der hat den Schaden angericht'. — Der Flieder war's: — Johannisnacht. — Nun aber kam Johannis-Tag: — jetzt schau'n wir, wie Hans Sachs es macht

Facsimile-Edition.	Second Printed Edition.
das Herz erwacht dem Ungeheuer,	dass er den Wahn fein lenken mag"
und weckt mit Pochen die Hand;	
die ballt sich schnell zur Faust,	
den Knüppel die gern umspannt;	
mit Faust und Knüppel da saus't,	
wer gern als tapfer bekannt:	
und will's der Wahn gesegnen,	
nun muss es Prügel regnen,	
mit Hieben, Stoss' und Dreschen,	
den Wuthesbrand zu löschen.	
Ein Koboldwahn. — Johannisnacht! —	
Nun aber, kam Johannis-Tag:	
jetzt schau'n wir, wie Hans Sachs es macht,	
dass er den Wahn fein lenken kann" [1])	
58. „Steh'n sie nun so in hohem Ruf"	237. „Steh'n sie nun in so hohem Ruf."

WALTHER'S DREAM-SONG.

59. „Fern meiner Jugend gold'nem Thoren zog ich einst aus, in Betrachtung ganz verloren: väterlich Haus,	239. „Morgenlich leuchtend in rosigem Schein, von Blüth' und Duft geschwellt die Luft, voll aller Wonnen nie ersonnen

---

1) This is a judicious omission. The figure in the Facsimile is carried out too far to accord with our literary taste, to say the least, and it is certainly too complex to be followed in singing.

Facsimile-Edition.	Second Printed Edition.
kindliche Wiege,	ein Garten lud mich ein
lebet wohl! ich eil', ich fliege	Gast ihm zu sein.
einer neuen Welt nun zu Stern	Wonnig entragend dem selbigen Raum
meiner einsam trauten Nächte	bot gold'ner Frucht
leuchte mir klar,	heilsaft'ge Wucht
dass mein Pfad zum Glück mich brächte,	mit holdem Prangen dem Verlangen
mütterlich wahr	an duft'ger Zweige Saum
helle mein Auge	herrlich ein Baum.
dass es treu zu finden tauge	
was mein Herz erfüll' mit Ruh'	
60. Abendlich	Sei euch vertraut
sank die Sonne nieder:	welch' hehres Wunder mir gescheh'n:
goldene Wagen	
auf den Bergen reihten sich;	an meiner Seite stand ein Weib,
Thürme und Bogen	
Häusser, Strassen breiten sich;	so schön und hold ich nie geseh'n,
durch die Thore zog ich ein, dünkte mich	gleich einer Braut
ich erkenn' sie wieder;	umfasste sie sanft meinen Leib;
auch der alte Flieder	
lud mich ein sein Gast zu sein;	mit Augen winkend,
auf die müden Glieder	die Hand wies blinkend,
labendlich	was ich verlangend begehrt,
goss er Schlaf mir aus, —	die Frucht so hold und werth
gleich wie im Vaterhaus —	vom Lebensbaum.
Ob ich die Nacht	
doch wohl geträumt hab', ob gewacht?	
Traum	Abendlich glühend in himmlischer Pracht
meiner thörig gold'nen Jugend,	
wurdest du wach	verschied der Tag,
durch der Mutter zarte Tugend?	wie dort ich lag;

Facsimile-Edition.
winkt sie mir nach,
folg' ich und fliege
über Stadt und Länder herein
zur Wiege,
wo mein die Traute harrt.
Kaum
dass ich nah zu sein ihr glaube,
blendend und weiss
schwebte sie auf als zarte
Taube,
pflückt dort ein Reis,
ob meinem Haubte
hält sie's kreisend, dass ich's
raubte
in holder Gegenwart.
Morgenlicht
dämmert da wieder
scherzend und spielend
Täubchen immer ferner wich
fliegend und zielend
zu den Thürmen lockt es'
mich;
flatternd über Häuser hin
setzte sich
auf dem Haus, dem Flieder
gegenüber, nieder,
dass ich dort das Reis gewinn;
und den Preis der Lieder.
Morgenlich
hab' ich das geträumt;
nun sagt mir ungesäumt,
was wohl am Tag
das holde Traum bedeuten
mag?
61. Freund! eure Mutter rieth
euch wahr.

Second Printed Edition.
aus ihren Augen
Wonne zu saugen,
Verlangen einz'ger Macht
in mir nur wacht. —

Nächtlich umdämmernd der
Blick sich mir bricht;
wie weit so nah'
beschienen da
zwei lichte Sterne
aus der Ferne
durch schlanke Zweige Licht
hehr mein Gesicht.

Lieblich ein Quell
auf stiller Höhe dort mir
rauscht;
jetzt schwillt er an sein hold
Getön'
so süss und stark ich's nie
erlauscht:
leuchtend und hell
wie strahlen die Sterne da
schön:
zum Tanz und Reigen
in Laub und Zweigen
der gold'nen sammeln sich
mehr,
statt Frucht ein Sternenheer
im Lorbeerbaum." —

241. Freund, eu'r Traumbild
wies euch wahr;

Facsimile-Edition.	Second Printed Edition.
61. Tag, den ich kaum gewagt zu träumen, brachst du mir an in der Freundschaft [Freiheit] trauten Räumen? Ist es kein Wahn? Sie, die ich liebe die das Herz mir schwellt mit süssem Triebe, sie steht voll [im] Glanz vor mir? Sag' ist es nicht die weisse Taube, lieblich und treu, wie der Jugend holder Glaube? Ihr ohne Reu' ganz mich zu geben ihr zu weihen mein [all] Glück, mein [all] Heil, mein [und] Leben wie, Mutter, dankt' ich's dir? Sonniglich will sie mir erglänzen: nächtliche Schleier decken mehr die Augen nicht; heller und freier sah' ich nie ein Angesicht: ob dem Haupte ihr schwebt ein Reis; ob sie das bricht von dem Zweig des Lenzen huldvoll ohne Grenzen mir die Stirn' um Sanges-Preis hold damit zu kränzen?	252. Weilten die Sterne im lieblichen Tanz? So licht und klar im Lockenhaar, vor allen Frauen hehr zu schauen, lag ihr mit zartem Glanz ein Sternenkranz. — Wunder ob Wunder nun bieten sich dar: zwiefacher Tag ich grüssen mag' denn gleich zwei'n Sonnen reinster Wonnen der hehrsten Augen Paar nahm ich nun wahr. Huldreichstes Bild, dem ich zu nahen mich erkühnt: den Kranz, von zweier Sonnen Strahl zugleich verblichen und ergrünt, minnig und mild sie flocht ihn um's Haupt dem Gemahl. Dort Huld-geboren Nun Ruhm-erkoren giesst paradiesisches Lust

Facsimile-Edition.	Second Printed Edition.
Wonniglich schönster Lebenstraum! des Paradieses Baum, reichst du dies Reis, wohl unversehrt ich blühen weiss'" 68. „Lausch', Kind! das war ein Meisterlied." [Do not occur] 73. „Der Muth hat und Ver- stand" [Do not occur]	sie in des Dichter's Brust — im Liebestraum." — 252. „Lausch', Kind! das ist ein Meisterlied." 251. „Wach oder träum ich schon so früh? Das zu erklären macht mir Müh'." 258. „Der viel Muth hat und Verstand." 262. „Gott! ist der dumm! Er fällt fast um! — Still! macht keinen Witz: der hat im Rathe Stimm' und Sitz."

BECKMESSER'S PARODY.

76. Fern meiner Tugend gold'nen Thoren bog ich einst aus in Verachtung ganz verloren: Vater im Haus, Kind in der Wiege! lebet wohl, denn eilig pflüge ich mein neues Feld nun zu. — — — — — — Sonderbar! Hört ihr's? Wo will das 'naus? Er bog voll Verachtung der Tugend aus?	263. Morgen ich leuchte im rosigem Schein voll Blut und Duft geht schnell die Luft', — wohl bald gewonnen, wie zerronnen, — im Garten lud ich ein — garstig und fein. — — — — — — — Sonderbar! Hört ihr's? Wen lud er ein? Verstand man recht? Wie kann das sein?

Facsimile-Edition.	Second Printed Edition.
Beckmesser.	Beckmesser.

<table>
<tr><td>

Gern
auf der heilsam kraut'nen Fläche
deuchte mir dar
dass mein Pferd 's Genick mir bräche;
bitterlich gar
gellte mein Auge,
dass wie Brei es nimmt und Lauge,
und viel Schmerz ich füllt' ohn' Ruh'!

— — — — — — —

Schöner Werber! der dünkt mich was werth!
Bald fällt er wohl auch hier vom Pferd.

— — — — — — —

Habe Dich!
klang Gesumme wieder:
goldene Wagen
auf den Bergen ritten sie;
Würste und Magen
auf den Häusern brieten sie:
und mich Thoren zog man ein
tünchte mich;
ach! ich brenne nieder!
Brau't mir kalten Flieder!"

</td><td>

Wohn ich erträglich im selbigen Raum, —
hol' Gold und Frucht —
Bleisaft und Wucht: —
mich holt am Pranger,
der Verlanger, —
auf luft'ger Steige kaum —
häng' ich am Baum.

— — — — — — —

Schöner Werber! Der find't seinen Lohn:
bald hängt er am Galgen; man sieht ihn schon.

— — — — — — —

Heimlich mir graut —
weil hier es munter will hergeh'n: —
an meiner Leiter stand ein Weib.
sie schämt und wollt' mich nicht beseh'n.
Bleich wie ein Kraut —
umfasert mir Hanf meinen Leib; —
Die Augen zwinkend —
der Hund blies winkend —
was ich vor langem verzehrt, —
wie Frucht, so Holz und Pferd —
vom Leberbaum.

</td></tr>
</table>

Facsimile-Edition.	Second Printed Edition.
80. „doch wohlgelungen auch dieser Bar."	268. „doch wohl gereimt und singebar."

SACHS' CLOSING SPEECH.

82. Verliebt und sangevoll, wie ihr kommen nicht oft uns Junker hier von ihren Burgen und Staufen nach Nürnberg hergelaufen: vor ihrer Lieb' und Fang-Begier das Volk oft mussten schaaren wir: und findet sich das in Haufen gewöhnt sich's leicht an Raufen: Gewerke, Gilden und Zünfte hatten üble Zusammenkünfte (wie sich's auf gewissen Gassen noch neulich hat merken lassen!) In der Meister-Singer trauten Zunft kamen die Zünfte immer wieder zur Vernunft Dicht und fest an ihr so leicht sich nicht rütteln lässt; aufgespart ist euren Enkeln, was sie bewahrt. Welkt mancher Sitt' und mancher Brauch,	Habt Acht! Uns drohen üble Streich': — zerfällt erst deutsches Volk und Reich in falscher wälscher Majestät kein Fürst bald mehr sein Volk versteht:

Facsimile-Edition.	Second Printed Edition.
zerfällt in Schutt, vergeht in Rauch, —	und wälschen Dunst mit wälschem Tand
Lasst ab vom Kampf!	sie pflanzen uns in's deutsche Land.
nicht Donnerbüchs' noch Pulverdampf	Was deutsch und ächt wüsst' Keiner mehr,
macht wieder dicht, was nur noch Hauch!	Lebt's nicht in deutscher Meister Ehr'.
Ehrt eure deutschen Meister" u. s. w.	Drum sag' ich euch ehrt eure deutschen Meister" u. s. w.

The disparity between the two texts is striking.

The Street-fight has been made longer and more vivacious. The superiority of the new dream-song to the older one is also obvious. The older one is artificial in style and trivial in conception, displaying very little of the originality and elasticity of Wagner's genius. The same improvement is to be noticed in Beckmesser's song. In the Fac-simile the parody is a little too crass — not for the ordinary German comic opera, but for comic opera which aspires at the same time to be grand opera. One of the most essential improvements is however the variation of the Dream-song in its second rendition. In the Fac-simile, the song sung on the meadow differs from the one composed in the work-shop only by a few unimportant words.[1]) The version given in the printed edition is quite changed, thus relieving the almost unpardonable error of repeating a song of three long strophes word for word in the same act. There is one echo of the original Dream-song still in the printed edition, i. e., where Hans Sachs says (VII, 242):

„ein Täubchen zeigt' ihm wohl das Nest,"

an allusion which is only recognized in the light of the Facsimile.

II. THE TEXT OF THE SCORE.

Another text which offers room for comparison is that of

---
1) These words are indicated by brackets.

the score. The orchestration of the „Mastersingers" was finished by Wagner in Triebchen, near Lucerne, on the 17th of March, 1867.[1]) As fast as the score was complete, he sent it to his friend Hans von Bülow, who wrote the piano-score for it. The text of this score[2]) holds a middle position between that of the Fac-simile and of the printed edition. It repeats unchanged many lines of the Fac-simile, which are changed in the standard text. But there are other changes which occur for the sake of the euphony of the music alone. Many of these are trifling changes in order, e. g.:

Score-text.	Printed Text.
57. „dass Meistersinger ich heiss"	158. „dass ich Meistersinger heiss,"
67. „so musste ich wohl sinnen"	172. „so musst' ich fleizig sinnen."
75. „drum mocht' es euch"	175. „D'rum mocht's euch nie"

In other places there are omissions for the sake of the music, as:

369. „Wie? Schön! Dieser Unsinns-wust?"	265. „Wie? Schön dieses Lied, der Unsinns-Wust?

In the music the two words „Wie? Schön" are prolonged so that they take as much time as would the longer „Wie? Schön dieses Lied?"

Furthermore, there are a few absolute changes of the metre, in all cases from a more crowded to a more liesurely time. e. g.

76. „Wie wäre dann der Meister Urteil frei?"	173. „wie wär' dann der Meister Urtheil frei?"
150. „Damit ich dir die zieren Schuh' gefasst"	199. „damit ich die zieren Schuh' dir gefasst."

There is one omission in the score, i. e. of the lines (VII, 179):

„Meint, Junker, hier in Sang' und Dicht'
euch rechtlich unterweisen,

---
1) Glasenapp, II, 182 ff.
2) „Die Meistersinger. Klavierauszug von Tausig."

und wollt' ihr, dass in Zunftgericht
zum Meister wir euch kiesen."

On the other hand, it contains two lines not in the printed text, e. g.

Score-text.	Printed Text.
110. „Ortel. — Nichts weiter! Zum Schluss!"	187. [Does not occur.]
269. Eva. „Keiner wie du so hold zu werben weiss."	269. [Does not occur.]

The stage-directions are also much fuller in the score-edition than in the printed text, but the principal difference is in the Street-fight, which corresponds to no other version.

213. „Verfluchter Bursch!"	224. „Verfluchter Kerl!"
314. „'s giebt {Schlägerei / Keilerei"	224. „'s giebt Prügelei!"
214. „Ihr da, lasst los!	224. „Ihr da! Auseinander!"
215 ff. Magdalene. David! bist du toll? Himmel! welche Noth! Hör doch nur, David! So lass doch nur den Herren los! Er hat mir nichts gethan. So hör mich doch nur an! Ach welche Noth! David! So hör doch nur einmal! Herr Gott! Er hält ihn noch! Mein! David! ist er toll? Ach! Ach! David, hör'! 's ist Herr Heckmesser!	225 ff. Magdalene. — David! Beckmesser! — — — — — Ach Himmel! Meine Noth ist gross! David! so hör mich doch nur an! So lass' doch nur den Herren los! Er hat mir ja nichts gethan!
Die Nachbarn. Esel! Dummrian! Wird euch wohl bange? Hat euch die Frau gehetzt? Das für die Klage!	225. Die Nachbarn. — Euch gönnt ich's schon lange! Wird euch wohl bange? Das für die Klage! — Seht euch vor, wenn ich schlage!

<table>
<tr><td>Score-text.</td><td>Printed Text.</td></tr>
<tr><td>

Schaut wie es Prügel setzt!
Lümmel! Grobian!
Seht euch vor, wenn ich schlage!
Seid ihr noch nicht gewitzt?
Nun schlagt doch! Das sitzt!
Dass dich! Hallunke!
Gleich ein Donnerwetter träfe!
Wartet, ihr Racker!
Maassabzwacker!
Euch gönnt' ich's lang!
Racker! Zwacker!
Wird euch bang?
Wollt ihr noch mehr?
Packt euch jetzt heim,
sonst kriegt ihr's von der Frau!
Geht's euch was an, wenn ich nicht will?
Auf, scheert euch heim!
So gut wie ihr, bin Meister ich!
Schickt die Gesellen heim!
Dummer Kerl! Haltet's Maul!
Schlägt sie nieder! Wir weichen nicht!
Tuchscherer! Leinweber!
Immer 'ran!
Stemmt euch hier nicht mehr zu Hauf'!
Wacker zu! Immer d'rauf!
Scheert euch heim
Oder sonst wir schlagen drein.
Zünfte! Zünfte! Zünfte heraus!

</td><td>

Hat euch die Frau gehetzt?
Schau' wie es Prügel setzt! —
Seid ihr noch nicht gewitzt? —
So schlagt doch! — Das sitzt! —
Dass dich! Hallunke! —
Hie Färbertunke! —
Wartet, ihr Racker! —
Ihr Maassabzwacker! —
Esel! — Dummrian! —
Du Grobian! —
Lümmel du! —
Drauf und zu! —

</td></tr>
</table>

Score-text.	Printed Text.
Lehrbuben.	222. Lehrbuben.

Herbei! Herbei! 's giebt
Keilerei!
Sind die Schuster!
Nein, sind die Schneider!
Die Trunkenbolde!
Die Hungerleider!
Kennt man die Schlosser
nicht?
Sie haben's sicher angericht'!
Ich glaub', die Schmiede
werden's sein!
Ich kenn' die Schreiner dort!
Gewiss die Metzger sind's!
Hei! Schaut die Schäffler
dort beim Tanz!
Dort seh die Bader ich im
Glanz!
Krämer finden sich zur Hand
mit Gerstenstang' und Zuckerkand,
mit Pfeffer, Zimmt, Muscatennuss.
Sie riechen schön, und machen
viel Verdruss!
Sie riechen schön und bleiben
gern vom Schuss!
Meinst du damit etwa mich!
Halt's Maul!
Mein ich damit etwa dich?
Das sitzt!
Seht nur, der Has'! —
Hat überall die Nas'! —
Immer heran!
Hei! Nun geht's! Plautz! hast
du nicht geseh'n?

Kennt man die Schlosser nicht?
Die haben's sicher angericht'! —
Ich glaub' die Schmiede werden's sein. —
Die Schreiner seh' ich dort
beim Schein. —
Hei! Schau die Schäffler dort
beim Tanz. —
Dort seh die Bader ich im
Glanz. —
Krämer finden sich zur Hand
mit Gesterstang' und Zuckerkand;
mit Pfeffer, Zimmt, Muscatennuss.
Sie riechen schön,
sie riechen schön,
doch haben viel Verdruss,
und bleiben gern vom Schuss.—
Seht nur, der Hase
Hat üb'rall die Nase! —
Mein'st du damit etwa mich?
Mein' ich damit etwa dich?
Da hast's auf die Schnauze! —
Herr, jetzt setzt's Plautze! —
Hei! Krach! Hagelwetterschlag!
Wo das sitzt, da wächst
nichts nach!
Keilt euch wacker;
haut die Racker!
Haltet selbst Gesellen Stand;
wer da wich', 's wär wahrlich Schand'!

Score-text.	Printed Text.
Ha! nun geht's! Krach! Hageldonnerwetterschlag! Wo es sitzt, da wächst nichts sobald nach. Der hat's gekriegt! Jetzt fährt's hinein, wie Hagelschlag! Bald setzt es blut'ge Kopf', Arm' und Bein'! Dort der Pfister denkt daran! Der hat's genug! Scheer sich jeder heim Der nicht mit keilt! Immer lustig! keilt euch wacker! Haltet selbst Gesellen mutig Stand! Wer wich', 's wär' wahrlich eine Schand Nicht gewichen! Wacker drauf und d'ran! Wir stehen Alle wie ein Mann!	Drauf und dran! Wie ein Mann steh'n wir alle zur Keilerei!
Gesellen. — Heda! Gesellen 'ran! Dort wird mit Zank und Streit gethan! Da giebt's gewiss noch Schlägerei! Gesellen! haltet euch dabei! 'Sind die Weber! 'Sind die Gerber! Die Preisverderber! Dacht' ich mir's doch gleich! Spielen immer Streich! Gebt's denen scharf!	226. Gesellen. Heda! Gesellen 'ran! Dort wird mit Streit und Zank gethan. Da gibt's gewiss gleich Schlägerei; Gesellen, haltet euch dabei! 's sind die Weber und Gerber! — Dacht' ich's doch gleich! — Die Preisverderber! Spielen immer Streich'! — Dort den Metzger Klaus,

Score-text.	Printed Text.
Dort den Metzger Klaus kenn' ich heraus!	den kennt man heraus! — Schneider mit dem Bügel!
'S ist morgen der Fünfte!	Hei, hie setzt's Prügel!
'S brennt Manchem im Haus!	Gürtler! — Zinngiesser! —
Hei! Hier setzt's Prügel.	Leimsieder! — Lichtgiesser! —
Schneider mit dem Bügel!	Tuchscherer her! —
Zünfte heraus!	Leinweber her! —
Ihr da macht! Packt euch fort!	Hieher! Hieher!
Wir sind hier g'rad am Ort!	Immer mehr! Immer mehr!
Wolltet ihr etwa den Weg uns hier verwehren?	Nur tüchtig drauf! Wir schlagen los:
Macht Platz, wir schlagen drein!	jetzt wird die Keilerei erst gross! —
Gürtler! Spängler!	Lauft heim, sonst kriegt ihr's von der Frau;
Zinngiesser! Leimsieder!	hier giebt's nur Prügel-Färbeblau!
Lichtsieder!	Immer 'ran!
Nicht gewichen! Schlagt sie nieder!	Mann für Mann!
Tuchscherer! Leinweber! Immer 'ran!	Schlagt sie nieder! Zünfte! Zünfte! Heraus! —
Wir schlagen herein!	
Zünfte d'rauf und dran!	
Zunfte! Zünfte heraus!	
Die Meister.	221. Die Meister. —
Was giebt's denn da für Zank und Streit?	Was giebt's denn da für Zank und Streit?
Das tos't ja weit und breit!	Das tos't ja weit und breit!
Gebt Ruh' und scheert euch jeder gleich nach Hause heim, sonst schlag' ein Hageldonnerwetter drein!	Gebt Ruh' und scheer' sich Jeder heim, sonst schlag' ein Hageldonnerwetter drein!
Gebt Ruh' und scheer sich Jeder heim, sonst schlagen wir Meister selbst noch drein.	Stemmt euch hier nicht mehr zu Hauf', oder sonst wir schlagen d'rauf. —

Score-text.	Printed Text.
Die Nachbarinnen.	221. Die Nachbarinnen. —
Was ist das für Zanken und Streit?	Was ist denn da für Streit und Zank?
Da giebt's gewiss noch Schlägerei!	's wird einem wahrlich Angst und bang!
Wär' nur der Vater nicht dabei!	Da ist mein Mann gewiss dabei:
Da ist mein Mann gewiss dabei.	gewiss kommt's noch zur Schlägerei!
Ach, welche Noth!	Heda! Ihr dort unten,
Mein! seht nur dort!	so seid doch nur gescheit!
's wird einem wahrlich Angst und bang!	Seid ihr zu Streit und Raufen gleich alle so bereit!
Ei hört! Was will die Alte da?	Was für ein Zanken und Toben!
Heda! Ihr dort unten!	Da werden schon Arme erhoben!
so seid nur gescheit!	Hört doch! Hört doch!
Seid ihr denn Alle gleich zu Streit und Zank bereit?	Sei ihr denn toll?
Mein! Dort schlägt sich mein Mann!	Sind euch die Köpfe vom Weine noch voll!
Sind die Köpfe von Wein euch voll?	Zu Hilfe! Zu Hilfe!
Ach Gott! Säh' ich nur meinen Hans!	Da schlägt sich mein Mann!
Seht dort den Christian!	Der Vater! der Vater!
er walkt den Peter ab.	Sieht man das an?
Mein! dort den Michel seht!	Christian! Peter!
der haut dem Steffen eins!	Niklaus! Hans!
Der Vater! der Vater!	Auf! Schreit Zeter! —
Sie hauen ihn todt!	Hörst du nicht, Franz?
Peter! so höre doch!	Gott, wie sie walken!
Jesus! der Hans hat einen Hieb am Kopf.	's wackeln die Zöpfe!
Gott steh' uns bei, geht das noch lange hier so fort	Wasser her! Wasser her!
Hei! Mein Mann schlägt wacker auf sie drein!	Giesst's ihn auf die Köpfe!

Score-text.	Printed Text.
Gott! welche Höllennoth! Hört Keiner mehr sein Wort! Die Köpf' und Zöpfe wackeln hin und her! Welches Toben! Welches Krachen! So hört doch! Auf! schafft Wasser her! Wasser! Wasser! Wasser her! Da giesst's auf die Köpf hinab! Wasser ist das Allerbeste für ihre Wuth! Auf! schreit zu Hilfe! Mord und Zeter herbei! Topf und Hafen! Krug und Kanne! Alles voll, und giesst's ihn' auf den Kopf!"	

CONCLUSION.

In conclusion we turn to a brief study of the language itself. As far as is consistent with modern demands, Wagner has tried to approach, both in metre and in vocabulary, the type of literary work of the time of which he writes, as represented by Hans Sachs. He has thus availed himself very largely of the „Knittelvers", a doggerel in which the bulk of Sachs' works are written, and which is familiar to modern ears through „Faust". This verse is made still more effective by frequent ellipsis of inflectional endings and of prefixes, a device quite in line with Sachs' style. Take as examples:

(VII, 197) „bin gar ein arm einfältig Mann."
(VII, 201) „Hab' heut' manch' Sorg' und Wirr' erlebt."
(VII, 266) „dass sie auch 'mal 'ne Ausnahm' verträgt."

A few old inflectional forms are introduced, which give an archaic flavor. Such are:

Femine Genitive and Dative singular in — en, e. g.

(VII, 184) „zu meiner Frauen Preis."
(VII, 216) „zur Gassen."
(VII, 252) „reinster Wonnen."
(VII, 268) „am lichten Tag der Sonnen."

Dative Plurals in — en, e. g.

(VII, 240) „Kinden."
(VII, 234) „Gemüthen."

Older conjugational forms are „erkiest" (VII, 218), and „genennt" (VII, 161). The latter is a provincial south German form. „Schuf" occurs always as the preterite of „schaffen" in the „Mastersingers".[1])

---

1) von Wolzogen: „Die Sprache in R. Wagner's Dichtungen", 90.

Wagner also prefers the older endings. „Melodie" is always written „Melodei" in this text, and occasionally we have the ending — nuss for the later — nis, as for example in „Ärgernuss" (VII, 224).

„Another characteristic, which is shared, however, by „Tristan", „Lohengrin", and the „Ring" 1) is the formation of feminines from verbal stems by the addition of — e, according to the Midale High German usage. Such forms are „Find'" (VII, 179). „Dicht'" (VII, 179), „Hoff'" (VII, 180), „Richt'" (VII, 181) and „Wirr'" (VII, 201). The reason is probably a distaste for bringing the heavier — schaft, — heit, and — ung in verse intended for singing.

We have also archaic forms without Umlaut, as „spat" (VII, 203, 234), beruck' (VII, 229), „hochgelahrt" (VII, 187) and „bass" (VII, 235).

We note also the arbitrary insertion of an e in several words, as is common in Hans Sachs, for example, „Mägdelein" (VII, 220), „Kindelein" (VII, 222), „liebelich" (VII, 230), „Nürenberg" (VII, 235), „singebar" (VII, 238).

These is occasionally an adverb in — e, as. „balde" (VII, 191), „geschwinde" (VII, 207).

There are also several archaic constructions, for example:

(VII, 158) „Das macht, weil sein Meister ein Schuster." This is a very common construction in the sixteenth century, occurring frequently in Luther, but is now comparatively rare.

(VII, 255) „Morgen voller Sterne."
„This construction occurs now only in the expression, „ein Himmel voller Geigen". In the first part of Goethe's Faust we have still an example in his „Himmel voller Sterne".2)

Another construction which Wagner uses freely and which also often occurs in „Faust" is that of a genitive absolute instead of a prepositional construction. Examples are:

(VII, 158) „Mein Herz, sel'ger Gluth."
(VII, 234) „wie friedsam, treuer Sitten."

---

1) von Wolzogen, 93 f.
2) Goethe: „Werke, Weimar-Ausgabe", XIV, 186.

(VII, 241) „Verlangen, einziger Macht."
(VII, 261) „einer Quelle edler Welle."
This construction is prone to occur in lyric parts of the drama.
There is quite a list of words which are either obsolete, or obsolete in the sense in which Wagner uses them. Of these may be mentioned:
(VII, 153) „Held" in the general sense of man.
(VII, 181) „zweenen."
(VII, 190) „Recke."
(VII, 218) „Beding."
(VII, 222) „Vergunst", „gewunst".
(VII, 223) „blusen" (= „blühen").
(VII, 229) „eilfe".
(VII, 229) „Jungfer" (in address obsolete. Wagner gives on page 193 the form „Jumbfer", philologically more correct than the usual form).

Forms which are dialectic in South German are:
(VII, 235) „Grüss Gott."
(VII, 192) „Schätzel."
(VII, 174) „Ade."
(VII, 166) „Geflunker."
(VII, 156) „Mein sagt!"
(VII, 216) „Schmierich."
(VII, 234) „Schmerz-Gekreisch."

„Ohrgeschinder" (VII, 185), „Geschlamb und Geschlumbfer" (VII, 193) are dialectical neologisms of Wagner's own. Words similar to these occur in Bavarian, but not these exact forms.

Riming couplets and alliterative couplets, both so characteristic of Hans Sachs' writings, occur frequently, for example:

(Riming Couplets.)
(VII, 157) „Gut und Blut."
(VII, 172) „geh' und steh'."
(VII, 254) „Lug und Trug."

(Alliterative Couplets.)
(VII, 153) „Küch' und Keller."
(VII, 153) „Schrein und Schrank."
(VII, 168) „Nenn' und Nam'."

(VII, 171) „Kling und Klang'."
(VII, 189) „Flug und Flucht."
(VII, 196) „still und stumm."
(VII, 213) „Schuh' und Stiefeln."
(VII, 218) „glatt und gut."
(VII, 253) „Topf und Tellern."
Alliteration outside of these couplets is very marked in this text, as in all of Wagner's later librettos. A so common device needs however no examples.

The uncouth and false rimes are very cleverly made to indicate the archaic and dialectic coloring of the poem. In Sachs are to be found just such rude rimes as:
(VII, 223) „heut' gern: hungern."
(VII, 264) „Singer: überspring' er."
(VII, 164) „Junker: Sprung er."
(VII, 185) „Ohrgeschinder: dahinter."
(VII, 198) „konnt' er's: besonders."

Other rimes indicate the dialectical pronunciation of vowels and consonants, as:
(VII, 157) „Küch: dich."
(VII, 164) „Heut': freit."
(VII, 88) „Melodei: Mischgebräu."
(VII, 234) „Dreschen: löschen!
(VII, 191) „neu: Mai."
(VII, 235) „Nürenberg: Werk."
(VII, 268) „bunter: Wunder."
(VII, 267) „Pfad: genaht."

There are also several identical rimes, as:
(VII, 179) „Vogelgesang: Gesang."
(VII, 188) „Übermacht: macht."
(VII, 183) „wall't: Allgewallt."
(VII, 248) „Theurer: Abenteurer."
which have likewise their prototypes in Hans Sachs.

The rime wich Wagner introduces so often:
„Sachs: blüh' und wachs",
is the closing rime of of a great number of Hans Sachs' poems, and is therefore most characteristic.

The other rime:
„Schuh: Poet dazu"
originated in the well-known rime which was intended to ridicule Hans Sachs:
„Hans Sachs war ein Schuh-
Macher und Poet dazu."
It is either in ignorance of this origin that Wagner puts it twice in the mouth of Sachs, or perhaps the cobbler himself good-humoredly takes up the joke of his enemies.

In spite of these single touches, Wagner was master enough not to overload his text with peculiarities merely in order to show that he was familiar with his subject. It is remarkable how the spirit of Hans Sachs pervades the entire piece, although in the letter he is almost absent. There is a subtle essence of the old cobbler-poet diffused throughout Wagner's work which can only be detected by one who is familiar with both Masters.

BIBLIOGRAPHY.

Bayreuther Blätter, herausgeg. vom Allg. Richard Wagner-Verein, 18 Bde., Bayreuth, 1878—96.
Böhme, Franz M. See Erk.
Cornell, J. H. See Heintz.
A'Assailly, Octave: „Les Chevaliers-Poëtes de L'Allemagne." Paris, 1862.
Deinhardstein, Johann Ludwig: „Hans Sachs." Schauspiel in vier Aufzügen, herausg. v. Carl Friedrich Wittmann. (Universal-Bibliothek.) Leipzig.
Ellinger, Georg: „E. T. A. Hoffmann. Sein Leben und seine Werke." Hamburg und Leipzig, 1894.
Erk (Ludwig) und Böhme (Franz M.): „Deutscher Liederhort", 3 Bde. Leipzig, 1893/4.
Genée, Rudolph: „Hans Sachs und seine Zeit." Leipzig, 1894.
Germania, herausg. v. Pfeiffer, Bartsch and Behaghel. 37 Bde. Stuttgart und Wien, 1856—92.
Glasenapp, Carl Friedrich: „Richard Wagner's Leben und Wirken", 2 Bde. Cassel und Leipzig, 1876/7.
Goethe, Johann Wolfgang von: Werke, herausgegeben im Auftrage der Grossherzogin Sophie von Sachsen, 79 Bde. Weimar, 1887—96.
Grimm, Jacob: „Kleinere Schriften", 8 Bde. Berlin und Gütersloh, 1864—90.
— — „Über den altdeutschen Meistergesang." Göttingen, 1811.
Hagen, (Ernst) August: „Norica, das sind Nürnbergische Novellen aus alter Zeit." 6. Aufl. Leipzig, 1887.
Heintz, Albert: „The Mastersingers of Nuremberg by Richard Wagner." Translated from the 2nd German Edition by J. H. Cornell. New York, 1890.
Hoffmann, E. T. A.: „Gesammelte Schriften", 12 Bde. Berlin, 1857.
Horn, J. B. See Nord und Süd.
Kind, Friedrich: „Der Freischütz." Romantische Oper in drei Akten. Musik von Karl Maria von Weber. (Gustav Mode's Text-Bibliothek). Berlin.
Lortzing, Albert. See Reger.
Mey, Curt: „Der Meistergesang in Geschichte und Kunst." Karlsruhe, 1892.
Muncker, Franz: „Richard Wagner. Eine Skizze seines Lebens und Wirkens." 4. Aufl. (Bayerische Bibliothek.) Bamberg, 1891.

Nord und Süd. 76 Bde. Breslau, 1885—96.
Opitz, Martin: „Buch von der Deutschen Poeterey", 1624. (Abdruck in: Neudrucke deutscher Litteraturwerke des XVI. und XVII. Jahrhunderts.)
Pietsch, Paul: „Martin Luther und die hochdeutsche Schriftsprache."
Plate, Otto. See Strassburger Studien.
Puschman, Adam: „Grundtlicher Bericht des Deudschen Meistergesangs." Görlitz, 1571. (Abdruck in: Neudrucke deutscher Litteraturwerke des XVI. und XVII. Jahrhunderts.)
Ranisch, M. Salomon: „Historischkritische Lebensbeschreibung Hanns Sachsens." Altenburg, 1765.
Reger, Philipp. „Hans Sachs." Komische Oper in drei Akten. Musik von Albert Lortzing. (Gustav Mode's Text-Bibliothek.) Berlin.
Sachs, Hans: „Gesammelte Werke", herausg. von Adelbert von Keller. 17 Bde. Tübingen, 1870—88. (Bibliothek des Litterarischen Vereins in Stuttgart.)
Sachs, Hans: „Dichtungen", 3 Bde., herausg. v. Karl Goedecke. Leipzig, 1870. (Deutsche Dichter des sechszehnten Jahrhunderts.)
Schilter, Johann: „Thesaurus Antiquitatum Teutonicarum" u. s. w. 4 Bde. Ulm, 1728.
Strassburger Studien, herausg. v. Ernst Martin und Wilhelm Wiegand. 3 Bde. Strassburg 1883 - 88.
Tacitus, Cornelius: „Germania", herausg. v. Dr. Heinrich Schweizer-Sidler. 5. Aufl. Halle a. S., 1890.
Tausig, Karl: „Die Meistersinger von Nürnberg von Richard Wagner." Vollständiger Klavierauszug. Mainz.
Taylor, Bayard: „Studies in German Literature." New York, 1879.
Müller, Franz: „Die Meistersinger von Nürnberg." Ein Versuch zur Einführung in die gleichnamige Dichtung Richard Wagners. München, 1868.
Uhland, Ludwig: „Schriften zur Geschichte der Dichtung und Sage." 8 Bde. Stuttgart, 1865—73.
Urstisius, Christian: „Germanie historici illustres." 2 Bde. Frankfurt, 1770.
Wagenseil, Johann Christopher: „De Civitate Noribergensi Commentatio." Als Anhang desselben „Buch von der Meistersinger Holdseligen Kunst Anfang, Fortübung, Nutzbarkeiten und Lehr-Sätzen." Altdorf, 1691.
Wagner, (Wilhelm) Richard: „Die Meistersinger von Nürnberg". Facsimile-Ausgabe des Textes. Mainz, 1893.
— — „Gesammelte Schriften und Dichtungen." 10 Bde. Leipzig, 1888.
Walther von der Vogelweide, herausg. v. Karl Bartsch. 6. Aufl. Leipzig, 1880. (Deutsche Classiker des Mittelalters.)
Weber, Karl Maria von. See Kind.
Wilsing, Heinrich: „Die Meistersinger von Nürnberg. Einführung in Musik und Dichtung." 2. Aufl. Mainz, 1892.
Wolzogen, Hans von: „Die Sprache in R. Wagner's Dichtungen. Leipzig, 1878.

www.ingramcontent.com/pod-product-compliance
Lightning Source LLC
Chambersburg PA
CBHW031122160426
43192CB00008B/1083